CAMBRIDGE UNIVERSITY PRESS

CAMBRIDGE ENGLISH
Language Assessment
University of Cambridge

Cambridge English

OFFICIAL
CAMBRIDGE PREPARATION MATERIAL

FIRST 3

WITH ANSWERS

WITHDRAWN

D1613283

AUTHENTIC EXAMINATION PAPERS

Cambridge University Press
www.cambridge.org/elt

Cambridge Assessment English
www.cambridgeenglish.org

Information on this title: www.cambridge.org/9781108433730

© Cambridge University Press and UCLES 2018

It is normally necessary for written permission for copying to be obtained
in advance from a publisher. The sample answer sheets at the back of this
book are designed to be copied and distributed in class.
The normal requirements are waived here and it is not necessary to write to
Cambridge University Press for permission for an individual teacher to make copies
for use within his or her own classroom. Only those pages that carry the wording
'© UCLES 2018 Photocopiable' may be copied. Photocopiable

First published 2018

20 19 18 17 16 15 14 13 12 11 10 9 8 7 6 5 4 3

Printed in Great Britain by CPI Group (UK) Ltd, Croydon CRO 4YY

A catalogue record for this publication is available from the British Library

ISBN 978-1-108-43373-0 Student's Book with answers
ISBN 978-1-108-38078-2 Student's Book with answers with Audio
ISBN 978-1-108-43372-3 Student's Book without answers
ISBN 978-1-108-43374-7 Audio CDs (2)

The publishers have no responsibility for the persistence or accuracy of URLs
for external or third-party internet websites referred to in this publication, and
do not guarantee that any content on such websites is, or will remain, accurate
or appropriate. Information regarding prices, travel timetables, and other factual
information given in this work is correct at the time of first printing but the
publishers do not guarantee the accuracy of such information thereafter.

Contents

Introduction

This collection of four complete practice tests comprises papers from the *Cambridge English: First (FCE)* examination; students can practise these tests on their own or with the help of a teacher.

The *Cambridge English: First* examination is part of a suite of general English examinations produced by Cambridge English Language Assessment. This suite consists of five examinations that have similar characteristics but are designed for different levels of English language ability. Within the five levels, *Cambridge English: First* is at Level B2 in the Council of Europe's *Common European Framework of Reference for Languages: Learning, teaching, assessment*. It has also been accredited by Ofqual, the statutory regulatory authority in England, at Level 1 in the National Qualifications Framework. The *Cambridge English: First* examination is widely recognised in commerce and industry, and in individual university faculties and other educational institutions.

Examination	Council of Europe Framework Level	UK National Qualifications Framework Level
Cambridge English: Proficiency *Certificate of Proficiency in English (CPE)*	C2	3
Cambridge English: Advanced *Certificate in Advanced English (CAE)*	C1	2
Cambridge English: First *First Certificate in English (FCE)*	B2	1
Cambridge English: Preliminary *Preliminary English Test (PET)*	B1	Entry 3
Cambridge English: Key *Key English Test (KET)*	A2	Entry 2

Further information

The information contained in this practice book is designed to be an overview of the exam. For a full description of all of the above exams, including information about task types, testing focus and preparation, please see the relevant handbooks which can be obtained from Cambridge English Language Assessment at the address below or from the website at: www.CambridgeEnglish.org

Cambridge English Language Assessment
1 Hills Road
Cambridge CB1 2EU
United Kingdom

Telephone: +44 1223 553997
email: helpdesk@cambridgeenglish.org

The structure of *Cambridge English: First* – an overview

The *Cambridge English: First* examination consists of four papers.

Reading and Use of English   1 hour 15 minutes
This paper consists of **seven parts**, with 52 questions. For Parts 1 to 4, the test contains texts with accompanying grammar and vocabulary tasks, and separate items with a grammar and vocabulary focus. For Parts 5 to 7, the test contains a range of texts and accompanying reading comprehension tasks.

Writing   1 hour 20 minutes
This paper consists of **two parts** which carry equal marks. In Part 1, which is **compulsory**, candidates have to write an essay of between 140 and 190 words, giving their opinion in response to a task. In Part 2, there are three tasks from which candidates choose one to write about. The range of tasks from which questions may be drawn includes an article, an email/ letter, a report and a review. In this part, candidates have to write between 140 and 190 words.

Listening   40 minutes (approximately)
This paper consists of **four parts**. Each part contains a recorded text or texts and some questions, including multiple-choice, sentence completion and multiple-matching questions. Each text is heard twice. There is a total of **30 questions**.

Speaking   14 minutes
This paper consists of **four parts**. The standard test format is two candidates and two examiners. One examiner takes part in the conversation while the other examiner listens. Both examiners give marks. Candidates will be given photographs and other visual and written material to look at and talk about. Sometimes candidates will talk with the other candidate, sometimes with the examiner, and sometimes with both.

Grading

Candidates will receive a score on the Cambridge English Scale for each of the four skills and Use of English. The average of these five scores gives the candidate's overall Cambridge English Scale score for the exam. This determines what grade and CEFR level they achieve. All candidates receive a Statement of Results and candidates who pass the examination with Grade A, B or C also receive the *First Certificate in English*. Candidates who achieve Grade A receive the *First Certificate in English* stating that they demonstrated ability at Level C1. Candidates who achieve Grade B or C receive the *First Certificate in English* certificate stating that they demonstrated ability at Level B2. Candidates whose performance is below B2 level, but falls within Level B1, receive a *Cambridge English* certificate stating that they have demonstrated ability at Level B1. Candidates whose performance falls below Level B1 do not receive a certificate.

   For further information on grading and results, go to the website (see page 4).

Test 1

READING AND USE OF ENGLISH (1 hour 15 minutes)

Part 1

For questions **1–8**, read the text below and decide which answer (**A**, **B**, **C** or **D**) best fits each gap. There is an example at the beginning (**0**).

Mark your answers **on the separate answer sheet**.

Example:

0 **A** gather   **B** produce   **C** find   **D** gain

0	A	B	C	D
	▭	▭	▭	▬

Alfred Wainwright

Alfred Wainwright came from a relatively poor family but managed to **(0)** .... qualifications in accountancy. However it is not for his skill in accountancy that he is **(1)** .... but for his pictorial guidebooks to the English Lake District.

The Lake District is in the north-west of England and **(2)** .... an area of some 2,292 square kilometres. As its name **(3)** .... , it is an area of lakes and mountains. Alfred first went there on a walking holiday in 1930 and immediately fell in love with the area.

He **(4)** .... the Lake District into seven parts and wrote a guide for each of them. The guides **(5)** .... entirely of copies of his hand-written manuscripts. All have descriptions of walks with hand-drawn maps and sketches of views from the summits of the different mountains. He intended the books to be just for his own personal **(6)** .... but was eventually **(7)** .... to publish them. They are beautiful books which **(8)** .... as popular as ever.

1	**A**	reminded	**B**	recollected	**C**	referred	**D**	remembered
2	**A**	reaches	**B**	extends	**C**	ranges	**D**	covers
3	**A**	implies	**B**	represents	**C**	proves	**D**	means
4	**A**	distributed	**B**	assigned	**C**	divided	**D**	allocated
5	**A**	involve	**B**	consist	**C**	include	**D**	contain
6	**A**	application	**B**	use	**C**	employment	**D**	practice
7	**A**	persuaded	**B**	impressed	**C**	caused	**D**	influenced
8	**A**	stay	**B**	keep	**C**	continue	**D**	remain

Part 2

For questions **9–16**, read the text below and think of the word which best fits each gap. Use only **one** word in each gap. There is an example at the beginning (**0**).

Write your answers **IN CAPITAL LETTERS on the separate answer sheet**.

Example: | **0** | T | O | | | | | | | | | | | | | | | | |

The origin of coins

According **(0)** .... the Greek historian Herodotus (484–425 BC), the Lydian people were the first to use metallic coins. In fact, these earliest coins were made out **(9)** .... electrum, a naturally-occurring mixture of gold and silver. The coins were first produced in the seventh century BC with a design on **(10)** .... side only; the other was marked with simple punches. Each coin was assigned a value in units. Some coins were inscribed with names in Lydian script, but it is unclear **(11)** .... these are names of kings or just of rich men who produced the coins. **(12)** .... of the irregular size and shape of the coins, it must **(13)** .... been difficult to tell one **(14)** .... another, especially some of the smaller ones. Thus, many costs were expressed **(15)** .... terms of the total weight of the coins required and transactions were completed by weighing the coins used together, **(16)** .... than counting individual ones.

Part 3

For questions **17–24**, read the text below. Use the word given in capitals at the end of some of the lines to form a word that fits in the gap **in the same line**. There is an example at the beginning (**0**).

Write your answers **IN CAPITAL LETTERS on the separate answer sheet**.

Example: | 0 | | A | C | T | I | V | I | T | Y | | | | | | | | | |

Play

Play is an (**0**) .... that all children take part in, whether alone or with   **ACTIVE**

others. In fact, play offers a wide (**17**) .... of benefits for children   **VARY**

and is vital for a child's learning and (**18**) .... development. It   **EMOTION**

is central to the formation of a child's personality and can help to

increase the knowledge children need to cope with the challenges

they encounter in school and at home. Play enables children to realise

their potential and to find solutions to problems, thus allowing them to

experience the (**19**) .... that success brings.   **SATISFY**

Experts tell us that it is (**20**) .... to overestimate the   **POSSIBLE**

(**21**) .... of play as it is probably the most effective way that   **IMPORTANT**

children have of trying out and mastering new skills. By opening

children's minds to (**22**) .... and imagination, play is indeed a good   **CREATE**

(**23**) .... for life.   **PREPARE**

However, as far as children themselves are concerned, the only value

of play is quite simply in the fun and (**24**) .... that it gives them.   **PLEASE**

Part 4

For questions **25–30**, complete the second sentence so that it has a similar meaning to the first sentence, using the word given. **Do not change the word given.** You must use between **two** and **five** words, including the word given. Here is an example (**0**).

Example:

0 A very friendly taxi driver drove us into town.

DRIVEN

We .... a very friendly taxi driver.

The gap can be filled by the words 'were driven into town by', so you write:

Example: | **0** | *WERE DRIVEN INTO TOWN BY*

Write **only** the missing words **IN CAPITAL LETTERS on the separate answer sheet.**

---

25 Martin never goes to bed without having a shower first.

HAS

Martin always .... to bed.

26 Tina was too frightened to stay in the house on her own.

BEEN

Tina would have stayed in the house on her own .... so frightened.

27 It will not be possible to buy tickets for the match until next Monday.

SALE

Tickets for the match will .... until next Monday.

28 The only vegetable that Helen dislikes is cabbage.

VEGETABLES

Helen .... from cabbages.

29 When Alex has finished his essay, a friend is going to check the spelling for him.

CHECKED

When Alex has finished his essay, he is going to .... a friend.

30 'I'm sorry to disturb you when you're so busy,' said Tom.

EXCUSE

'Please .... you when you're so busy,' said Tom.

Part 5

You are going to read part of the introduction to a cookery book called *In Search of Total Perfection* by Heston Blumenthal. For questions **31–36**, choose the answer (**A, B, C** or **D**) which you think fits best according to the text.

Mark your answers **on the separate answer sheet**.

When my first cookery programme *In Search of Perfection* first came out, I had no idea how it would be received by the viewers and the press. There had been plenty of talk going round at the time about the food 'revolution' sweeping through Britain, and I was certain that we'd produced a series of programmes that made a genuinely innovative contribution to that, but still the question worried me: would people appreciate an approach to cooking that involved not just techniques but also history, nostalgia and science? I watched the first programme in a mixed state of joy and fear.

I needn't have worried. The subsequent success of the show paved the way for all sorts of other fascinating projects, including a book based on my experiences at the restaurant I own. In each project there is a sense of being on a journey, be it into the past, into the mind, or into cookery techniques. I then wrote several books in a series called 'Perfection', each one accompanying its own TV programme of the same name. In these, however, the journey was often a very physical one, with passports and suitcases and itineraries. *In Search of Total Perfection* is the latest in the series, and in it you'll zigzag the globe in order to meet some extraordinary artisans, such as a man who finds his true purpose in creating a golden pasta that tastes better than any other. These people have spent decades pursuing their own ideals of perfection.

Perfection is, of course, highly subjective. Even the seemingly simple task of choosing which dishes to include in the series turned out to be a nightmare, and I knew I was bound to upset many people by leaving out their particular favourite. 'Where's steak and kidney pie and bread and butter pudding?' I could imagine people saying. Nevertheless, after shutting ourselves away in a meeting room and agreeing not to emerge until we had come up with a suitable list, the TV production team and I eventually had something for everyone.

This reinforced my opinion that each of us has our own idea of what constitutes perfection, drawing heavily on a highly personalised mix of emotions, memories and surroundings. Despite the book's title, *In Search of Perfection*, I knew from the outset that I wouldn't be claiming the recipes were in any way 'definitive'. But I reckoned that, by using my technical skill and scientific knowledge, by talking to food producers and artisans and chefs and their customers, I could pin down some of the things that made these dishes work.

While the dictionary defines 'perfection' as the state of being perfect, it also offers a second definition of equal importance to this book: honing through gradual experimentation. *line 62* Trying out ideas and then revising them until you arrive at something uniquely wonderful. The TV series gave me the opportunity to get out and look into all sorts of foods, people and places I'd never encountered before in any restaurant, and I was as excited about that as I *line 68* was about the chance to explore memory and nostalgia in food because I started out in this business in exactly the same way.

Searching out the best ingredients for the recipes took me all over the globe. Among my adventures were: being taken with great solemnity and assurance to a canning factory that turned out to be processing completely the wrong sort of tomato, and visiting a dairy farm whose standards fell so far short of perfection that we had to stop filming there! Refining the technique for each recipe, I ended up hand-milking a cow and then using dry ice to turn the milk into ice cream, cooking chicken breasts in a hospital scanning machine and nearly burning my house down in an effort to get the oven hot enough for a proper Neapolitan-style pizza.

31 In the second paragraph, Heston implies that the books in the 'Perfection' series

  A had a more international focus than his first book.
  B strongly developed the psychological aspect of the subject.
  C feature some characters who re-appeared in different books.
  D were less successful than the TV programmes that went with them.

32 What did Heston think about the meeting to discuss the 'Perfection' series?

  A It was useful in highlighting some practical problems.
  B It resulted in a very strange decision.
  C It should have been more productive.
  D It was demanding but efficient.

33 What does Heston imply about the recipes in his new book?

  A They vary considerably from the versions that inspired them.
  B They could be developed further in the future.
  C The final wording of them was easy to come up with.
  D The selection is not necessarily one he would have made himself.

34 What does 'honing' in line 62 tell us about the recipes?

  A They can never be completely perfect.
  B They are regarded by Heston as being experimental.
  C They serve another significant purpose in Heston's book.
  D They have been worked on and improved over a period of time.

35 What does 'that' refer to in line 68?

  A being willing to try out new things
  B learning the trade in a particular restaurant
  C exploring the relationship between food and the past
  D wondering about the importance of food in people's lives

36 Heston says that during his travels around the globe, he

  A had to be resourceful and adaptable.
  B narrowly avoided disaster on several occasions.
  C was forever solving problems caused by other people's incompetence.
  D had to respect an unusual local custom.

Part 6

You are going to a read a newspaper article about observing marine creatures called manatees. Six sentences have been removed from the article. Choose from the sentences **A–G** the one which fits each gap (**37–42**). There is one extra sentence which you do not need to use.

Mark your answers **on the separate answer sheet.**

Swimming with Manatees, Florida's Gentle Giants

When most people flock to the famous amusement parks in Orlando, Florida, they miss some of the natural wonders the State has to offer. It was in Citrus County on the beautiful west coast of Florida that we went to see the manatee, an amazing mammal that occupies coastal waters and rivers.

Our days started early in the morning at Homosassa Springs, as this is the perfect time to snorkel with the manatees before they get tired of visitors. We boarded a pontoon boat with Captain Traci Wood from Native Vacations. Having spotted two manatees just below the water, Captain Traci stopped the boat as the duo slowly glided towards us. | **37** | Our boat was soon surrounded by other members of this gentle species.

Soon we resumed our journey. Within a few minutes Captain Traci stopped the boat again and we were given instructions. Whatever you do, she said, remember the three golden rules: minimize splash noise; act with very slow movements; and when you touch one of these friendly, gentle gray giants on the back or stomach, never touch with more than one hand at a time. The Endangered Species Act forbids touching a manatee unless it touches you first, and they will let you know. The protection of this endangered species is taken very seriously. For children, there is absolutely no chasing or riding the manatees. | **38** | Most Homosassa manatees are very social and will come to you.

The next day, at Three Sisters Springs, we entered the water very slowly, trying to keep down the amount of thick, muddy sediment rising from the bottom of the river. | **39** | This meant swimming with the manatees was not at all difficult or intimidating. We saw young children as well as seniors in the water and there was an abundant feeling of energy and curiosity among us all.

Manatees are strictly herbivores, and they eat a great variety of species, including water hyacinth and water lettuce. They're very big, measuring 3 to 5 metres and weighing as much as 1,600 kilos. | **40** | Manatees are of course wild creatures, although when face to face with them, you're unlikely to feel any fear.

Since not all visitors want to get nose-to-nose with the manatees, non-swimmers can also view them at Homosassa Springs State Wildlife Park. The park provides a wonderful home for some manatees. | **41** | They are well looked after by people who really understand them. The park also serves as a research and observation center, offering three daily educational programs to the public.

From December to March, groups of manatees escape the cold winter ocean and bask in the warm waters near power plants and coastal springs that stay about 23 degrees year-round. Snorkelers, divers and swimmers come to Florida from all over the world for a chance to swim or interact with the docile manatee in its natural environment, rich in marine vegetation. | **42** | So the manatees arrive every year by the hundreds to find warmth, nourishment and maybe, just maybe, to visit us, the curious humans.

A   The truth is, swimming with manatees is a life-altering experience.

B   Those that have been injured or orphaned will also spend their lives there since they are unable to survive in the wild.

C   But this won't diminish the experience in the least.

D   This abundant source of food makes this area an ideal habitat for the manatees.

E   This was to avoid disturbing some of the manatees who were still sleeping while others were slow-paddling around.

F   They used their paddle-like tails to propel themselves, steering with their flippers, gracefully moving their bodies through the water in our direction.

G   Despite this, they look very cute.

Part 7

You are going to read an article about four people who set up local environmental projects. For questions **43–52**, choose from the people (**A–D**). The people may be chosen more than once.

Mark your answers **on the separate answer sheet**.

___

Which person

accepted that the attitudes of local people might be impossible to change?	43	
included a useful additional feature on a product?	44	
co-operated with others to develop the initial idea?	45	
had to convince local people to take part in an experiment?	46	
managed to get products sold in other countries?	47	
received formal recognition for a project's achievements?	48	
realised that it wasn't possible to use ideas that had worked elsewhere?	49	
saw that a traditional way of life was under threat?	50	
created an example that people in different places were able to follow?	51	
used materials that they recycled?	52	

Local environmental heroes

Four innovators who founded local conservation projects

A Evans Wadongo

Like many Kenyans, Evans Wadongo grew up studying by the light of a kerosene lamp. Bad for his eyes, the lamps also produced harmful fumes that made him cough. So, Evans designed a cleaner sun-powered alternative. Instead of importing solar technology from a mass-producing country, he set up the Use Solar initiative, which trained youngsters to manufacture special solar-powered lamps, using locally-sourced scrap metal and fragments of solar panels. A USB port, built into the base, offered an easy way to charge phones and radios. The lamps were then given to local groups, who used the money they saved on kerosene to set up small businesses such as poultry farming or beekeeping. Evans says that getting finance for the project was a challenge due to its long-term nature. Each lamp costs $25, which covers materials, training and distribution. The groups used money from their successful businesses to buy more lamps.

B Alasdair Harris

Coastal communities in south-western Madagascar have lived by fishing for more than a thousand years. But when biologist Alasdair Harris visited the region, he found them struggling to sustain themselves because population increases had diminished local fish stocks. Unsurprisingly, people had mixed feelings when he suggested closing one of the local fishing grounds, but agreed to a three-month trial. When it was re-opened, they caught a staggering 1,200 kg of octopus in one day and the community could see the benefit of looking after their resources. Others soon took up the model and the country now boasts hundreds of marine areas, monitored and protected by local people. Organisations in neighbouring countries have begun to replicate the model, as recognition grows for the importance of locally initiated conservation. 'We need a radically new approach,' Alasdair says, 'that's why we do this work.'

C Nam Nguyen

Although much of Vietnam's population lives in rural areas, its two major cities are increasingly affected by traffic and pollution. Ride-sharing was a relatively new concept when Nam Nguyen founded his Hanoi-based ride-sharing website. Initially, he intended to make a free network where people could share vehicles and contribute to protecting the environment. 'I tried to learn the model from European schemes, but they didn't really work here. Private vehicles are a source of pride for many city dwellers, who rely on them to visit their families in the provinces. They wouldn't give them up easily.' He realised he'd have to form a business plan to help finance and promote the idea. So, Nam designed a taxi-sharing service whose profits could support the ride-sharing enterprise he had initially imagined. 'The taxi service has become our main revenue stream. It allows the ride-sharing network to continue to grow.'

D Bernice Dapaah

About to graduate with a business administration degree but facing a tough job market in Ghana, Bernice Dapaah joined forces with some engineering students to create an innovative product from bamboo, an abundant crop in Ghana. They make strong, lightweight and durable bikes out of bamboo, using an ever-growing team of young people specially trained for the role. The project has serious green credentials, too: not only are the bikes an affordable, environmentally sound alternative to cars, but bamboo is fast-growing, produces up to 35% more oxygen than other trees and helps to prevent soil erosion, a significant cause of concern for farmers. It's an idea so brilliant the team went on to win ten international awards. The initiative had soon sold over a thousand bikes, including exports, allowing new workshops to be set up. The idea is that each employee, once trained, can train and employ five others and bikes can be produced on a small scale all over Ghana.

WRITING (1 hour 20 minutes)

Part 1

You **must** answer this question. Write your answer in **140–190** words in an appropriate style **on the separate answer sheet**.

---

1   In your English class you have been talking about money for sports people. Now, your English teacher has asked you to write an essay.

Write your essay using **all** the notes and giving reasons for your point of view.

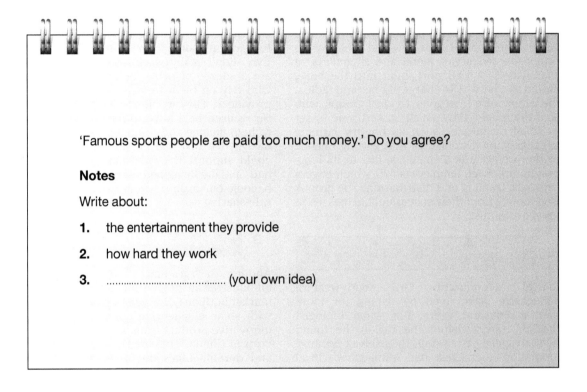

'Famous sports people are paid too much money.' Do you agree?

Notes

Write about:

1.   the entertainment they provide

2.   how hard they work

3.   ………………………………… (your own idea)

Part 2

Write an answer to **one** of the questions **2–4** in this part. Write your answer in **140–190** words in an appropriate style **on the separate answer sheet**. Put the question number in the box at the top of the answer sheet.

---

2   In your English class you have been discussing why parks and green spaces are important for people living in towns and cities. Now your English teacher has asked you to write a report.

In your report, you should:

- describe the parks and green spaces in your area
- recommend ways of improving these green spaces
- say why these improvements would have a positive effect on people's lives.

Write your **report**.

3   You see this advertisement in the online magazine *Global Food*:

> **Wanted: Restaurant reviewer**
>
> We are looking for someone to write reviews of restaurants in your area. You should:
>
> - be able to take photographs to go with your reviews
> - be interested in different types of food
> - have a good level of English.
>
> Write to the magazine editor, Phil Simms, explaining why you are suitable for the job.

Write your **letter of application**.

4   You see this notice in an English-language magazine:

> *Articles wanted*
>
> # Technology
>
> Which piece of technology would our lives be better without? Why?
>
> The best articles will be printed next month.

Write your **article**.

LISTENING (approximately 40 minutes)

Part 1

You will hear people talking in eight different situations.

For questions **1–8**, choose the best answer (**A**, **B** or **C**).

---

1   You hear a woman talking on the radio about an actor.

   What does the woman say about him?

   A   His acting has improved over the years.

   B   The media often criticise him unfairly.

   C   He gets fewer film roles than he deserves.

2   You hear a hairstylist talking about her career.

   She prefers working in the TV industry because she

   A   feels that her contribution is valued.

   B   is able to express her opinions freely.

   C   thrives on the creative challenge the work presents.

3   You hear a comedian called Geoff Knight talking on the radio about his profession.

   What does Geoff like his act to contain?

   A   stories that give people a surprise

   B   things that everybody can relate to

   C   material that nobody has used before

4   You hear a conversation between a customer and a coffee shop employee.

   What is the employee doing?

   A   waiting for a colleague's help

   B   excusing a colleague's inefficiency

   C   criticising a colleague's attitude

5   You hear a man telling a friend about an art exhibition.

What does he say about it?

A It was well attended.

B The lighting was effective.

C The catalogue was worth buying.

6   You overhear a man ringing a sports shop.

Why is he calling?

A to report an incident in the shop

B to make a special order

C to follow up an earlier query

7   You hear a man telling a friend about his work.

How does the man feel about his work?

A resentment of his colleague's success

B regret at the changes that have taken place

C frustration at his lack of progress

8   You hear two people talking about a country walk they're doing.

What do they agree about?

A It's much too long to complete.

B The path is very difficult to follow.

C They've chosen the wrong day to do it.

Part 2

You will hear a presentation given by a university student called Megan Rowlings about a forest survival course she went on in Australia. For questions **9–18**, complete the sentences with a word or short phrase.

Survival in the forest

It was Megan's **(9)** .... who told her about the survival course.

Megan particularly appreciated the course leader John's use of **(10)** ....

at stressful moments.

Megan said the assistant's knowledge of **(11)** .... was very useful during the course.

Megan was worried that her **(12)** .... would be a problem in doing some of the tasks.

John emphasised that when it comes to safety, **(13)** .... is the

most dangerous reaction.

Megan's teammates were grateful for the **(14)** .... which she'd brought with her.

Megan learned how to make a **(15)** .... from the material found in the forest.

Megan and her group were told they should only use water from

the **(16)** .... for drinking.

Megan found that making a **(17)** .... was hard for her.

Megan was surprised to find that the skill of **(18)** .... benefited her.

Part 3

You will hear five short extracts in which people talk about a problem they had in their first few weeks in a new job. For questions **19–23**, choose what problem (**A–H**) each speaker says they had. Use the letters only once. There are three extra letters which you do not need to use.

A   I made an embarrassing comment.

B   I didn't get on with my colleagues.

Speaker 1 | 19 |

C   I took on too much work.

Speaker 2 | 20 |

D   I didn't get enough support.

Speaker 3 | 21 |

E   I found the work too challenging.

Speaker 4 | 22 |

F   I was over-confident.

Speaker 5 | 23 |

G   I wasn't very punctual.

H   I was treated unreasonably.

Part 4

You will hear an interview with an international concert pianist called Karen Hong. For questions **24–30**, choose the best answer (**A**, **B** or **C**).

_____

24 Why does Karen keep practising pieces of music she knows well?

    A to keep her confidence levels high

    B to warm up before playing difficult new pieces

    C to make small improvements to her performance of them

25 What does Karen say about her mother?

    A She still tries to have an influence over Karen.

    B She shows her emotions much more than Karen's father.

    C She could have been a competent pianist herself.

26 Karen says that after winning a big competition, she began

    A to lose interest in music.

    B to take offence easily.

    C to doubt her talent.

27 Karen's decision to take a break from performing allowed her to

    A spend a lot of time on her own.

    B regain full physical health.

    C put a new management team in place.

28 When she was performing on television regularly, Karen enjoyed the idea that

    A she was bringing people from different countries closer together.

    B she was improving people's mood and energy levels.

    C she was taking classical music to new places and people.

29 What does Karen say about pop music?

    A It is suitable for people of all ages.

    B It makes little impression on her.

    C It affects teenagers' behaviour in different ways.

30 Karen believes that when dealing with young children who play music

    A praise should only be given where it is justified.

    B pushing them too hard will demotivate them.

    C it's a mistake to make them nervous about the end result.

SPEAKING (14 minutes)

You take the Speaking test with another candidate (possibly two candidates), referred to here as your partner. There are two examiners. One will speak to you and your partner and the other will be listening. Both examiners will award marks.

Part 1 (2 minutes)

The examiner asks you and your partner questions about yourselves. You may be asked about things like 'your home town', 'your interests', 'your career plans', etc.

Part 2 (a one-minute 'long turn' for each candidate, plus a 30-second response from the second candidate)

The examiner gives you two photographs and asks you to talk about them for one minute. The examiner then asks your partner a question about your photographs and your partner responds briefly.

Then the examiner gives your partner two different photographs. Your partner talks about these photographs for one minute. This time the examiner asks you a question about your partner's photographs and you respond briefly.

Part 3 (4 minutes)

The examiner asks you and your partner to talk together. They give you a task to look at so you can think about and discuss an idea, giving reasons for your opinion. For example, you may be asked to think about some changes in the world, or about spending free time with your family. After you have discussed the task for about two minutes with your partner, the examiner will ask you a follow-up question, which you should discuss for a further minute.

Part 4 (4 minutes)

The examiner asks some further questions, which leads to a more general discussion of what you have talked about in Part 3. You may comment on your partner's answers if you wish.

Test 2

READING AND USE OF ENGLISH (1 hour 15 minutes)

Part 1

For questions **1–8**, read the text below and decide which answer (**A**, **B**, **C** or **D**) best fits each gap. There is an example at the beginning (**0**).

Mark your answers on the **separate answer sheet**.

Example:

0 **A** ways   **B** methods   **C** manners   **D** types

0	A	B	C	D
	▬	▭	▭	▭

Tea bags

Over the centuries, tea has been made in many different **(0)** .... across the world. In the USA, until a little over a hundred years ago, dried tea was always sold and consumed as loose leaves. To make a drink, boiling water was poured over the tea leaves and **(1)** .... to stand while the water **(2)** .... the flavour of the leaves.

In 1908, Thomas Sullivan, a New York tea salesman, had the **(3)** .... idea of putting tea leaves in small silk bags to **(4)** .... as samples to potential customers. Sullivan **(5)** .... the tea to be removed from the bags before making a drink in the conventional manner. However, for the sake of **(6)** .... , his customers **(7)** .... up with the revolutionary practice of dipping the silk bag, contents and all, into boiling water. Cheap paper bags were introduced in the 1930s, completing the design of the modern tea bag. Today billions of **(8)** .... paper bags of tea are sold annually worldwide.

1	**A** set	**B** kept	**C** left	**D** saved
2	**A** immersed	**B** soaked	**C** filled	**D** absorbed
3	**A** sharp	**B** bright	**C** light	**D** keen
4	**A** put in	**B** give up	**C** hand out	**D** make over
5	**A** intended	**B** determined	**C** designed	**D** established
6	**A** satisfaction	**B** benefit	**C** convenience	**D** opportunity
7	**A** thought	**B** came	**C** started	**D** made
8	**A** distinct	**B** particular	**C** specific	**D** individual

Part 2

For questions **9–16**, read the text below and think of the word which best fits each gap. Use only **one** word in each gap. There is an example at the beginning (**0**).

Write your answers **IN CAPITAL LETTERS on the separate answer sheet.**

Example: | 0 | | A | R | E | | | | | | | | | | | | | | | |

Kangaroos

Kangaroos **(0)** .... found in the wild only in Australia and its surrounding islands. There are several species of kangaroo but the best known are the large red, grey and antilopine kangaroos. They all have large feet and extremely strong back legs as **(9)** .... as a long tail, and can grow up to 1.6 metres tall. They tend to jump rather **(10)** .... walk because their large feet make walking difficult.

The one fact that almost **(11)** .... knows about kangaroos is that young kangaroos, joeys, live in a kind of pocket at the front of their mother's body. Although they may come **(12)** .... of the pocket to play or explore, the pocket is **(13)** .... they live for many months after their birth.

Kangaroos feed on grasses, leaves, flowers and moss. They live in groups known **(14)** .... mobs and protect one **(15)** .... from danger. They present **(16)** .... serious threat to human beings because they rarely attack people, and only if provoked.

Part 3

For questions **17–24**, read the text below. Use the word given in capitals at the end of some of the lines to form a word that fits in the gap **in the same line**. There is an example at the beginning (**0**).

Write your answers **IN CAPITAL LETTERS on the separate answer sheet**.

Example: | **0** | V | A | R | I | E | T | Y | | | | | | | | | |

Bicycle racing

There is a wide **(0)** .... of different types of bicycle racing. A race **VARY**
may be an event held indoors over a relatively short distance, or
alternatively it can be outdoors and much longer, involving hundreds
of kilometres over a number of days. As the **(17)** .... of bicycle **POPULAR**
racing has grown worldwide, attention has focussed increasingly
on the **(18)** .... study of the sport and its many physical and **SCIENCE**
psychological **(19)** .... There seems to be agreement among **REQUIRE**
sports experts that competitive cycling, more than almost any other
sport, places **(20)** .... demands on the whole human body. **EXCEPT**

Successful participants in many sports can be a bit **(21)** .... or **FIT**
slightly overweight but nevertheless have sufficient **(22)** .... to **ABLE**
compensate for that. That is not true for serious cyclists who aim to
do well in competitions. They must show extraordinary dedication
to the sport. Many seem to have an **(23)** .... with it and an **OBSESS**
(24) .... of the hours and hours of practice necessary to achieve **ACCEPT**
success.

Part 4

For questions **25–30**, complete the second sentence so that it has a similar meaning to the first sentence, using the word given. **Do not change the word given**. You must use between **two** and **five** words, including the word given. Here is an example (**0**).

Example:

0   A very friendly taxi driver drove us into town.

DRIVEN

We .... a very friendly taxi driver.

The gap can be filled by the words 'were driven into town by', so you write:

Example:	0	WERE DRIVEN INTO TOWN BY

Write **only** the missing words **IN CAPITAL LETTERS on the separate answer sheet**.

---

25   John had never been in that part of the country before.

FIRST

It .... that John had ever been in that part of the country.

26   I wish I could play the guitar, but I can't.

ABLE

I would .... play the guitar, but I can't.

27   The public swimming pool didn't use to be so crowded.

THAN

The public swimming pool is .... to be.

28 Nobody knows for certain the depth of the water in the middle of the lake.

DEEP

Nobody knows for certain .... in the middle of the lake.

29 Although the room became quite noisy, the singer continued singing.

EVEN

The singer carried .... the room became quite noisy.

30 I have never seen an elephant as large as the one in the film.

SUCH

I haven't .... elephant as the one in the film.

Part 5

You are going to read an article about a man who makes guitars. For questions **31–36**, choose the answer (**A**, **B**, **C** or **D**) which you think fits best according to the text.

Mark your answers **on the separate answer sheet**.

The guitar maker

Jonny Kinkead, one of the best known makers of hand-crafted acoustic guitars in the UK, talks about his career.

As a boy, when Jonny Kinkead wasn't making things using the tools in his dad's garage, he was messing about with a guitar. And the two preoccupations have been his living for the past four decades: building steel-string, acoustic guitars by hand. 'The guitar still holds me in thrall,' he says. 'Making a sound out of planks of wood – it's amazing what you can do. By using different combinations of timber, for example, you get a different sound, and that is what musicians are interested in – a sound that can do what they want it to do.'

Jonny learned to play his brother's guitar when he was eleven. Then, when he was sixteen, he wanted to learn the bass guitar. 'Some people would have got a holiday job and saved up and bought one,' he says. 'But I was of a mindset that if you wanted something, you made it.'

Although the bass was the first instrument Jonny built from scratch, he and his brothers had long been doing essentially the same thing with other items. 'I made model boats and aeroplanes as a child, so I was familiar
line 25
with that process. My father had taught me and my brothers how to use tools, and we had free rein in the garage.' Jonny had also been customising and repairing instruments for his mates.

Jonny's bass guitar turned out well, but the idea of a career building guitars had yet to cross his mind. 'My ambition in those days was to be a sculptor,' he says. His interests evolved further and on finishing school, he chose to study architecture at university. Halfway through the course, however, he dropped out, but he left with a clearer idea of what he wanted to do and started to think seriously about guitar making. 'I was still interested in painting and sculpture but I realised that when you are building guitars you're actually

sculpting sound.' In addition he explains, 'I thought this might be more reliable than being an artist as it's craft-based.'

Ever since then, Jonny has made guitars for a living. For the first ten years, he supplemented his income by cleaning windows part-time. The first guitars he sold only went for the cost of the materials, but as he developed a reputation as one of the best guitar-makers around, he was able to charge a little more. But even now, almost forty years later, Jonny describes what he does as 'still scratching a living'. He admits he can never actually turn out more than ten guitars a year, which inevitably restricts his earnings.

In the early years, the key thing was to make the effort to get himself known. He would go to music festivals most weekends if he could and get musicians to try out his guitars and talk about him to their friends. He also had to learn how to price his instruments – when it came up in conversations with musicians, he hadn't got an answer because focusing on such things didn't come naturally to him.

Jonny believes developing a career is more straightforward for today's new guitar-makers in the UK. 'When I started it was hard because people thought that the guitars I was making were only made in America and that people in the UK didn't know how to make them. Now there is a culture of hand-making guitars that has grown up over the past 40 years in the UK. It is easier now for them,' he says. You may be able to learn valuable techniques in the classroom, Jonny concludes, but there is no substitute for trial and error, 'Make 100 guitars and you learn a lot.'

31 Why did Jonny choose to make a bass guitar for himself when he was a teenager?

    A   He regarded it as the natural thing to do.
    B   He saw it as good practice for making other guitars.
    C   He feared that he would never be able to buy one.
    D   He thought he could ensure it was in the style he wanted.

32 What does 'that process' in line 25 refer to?

    A   creating something from nothing
    B   working with his brothers
    C   doing things for friends
    D   getting tools ready

33 What does Jonny say about the architecture course he attended?

    A   It gave him the opportunity to explore different types of art.
    B   It provided him with ideas for guitar design.
    C   It enabled him to decide on a career path.
    D   It helped him become more independent.

34 What does Jonny suggest is the main reason for his low income?

    A   the cost of the materials he makes guitars with
    B   the small number of guitars that he produces
    C   the limited demand for hand-made guitars
    D   the competition between guitar-makers

35 What does Jonny say he found hard in his early years as a guitar-maker?

    A   deciding how much to charge for his guitars
    B   working out how to advertise his services
    C   building up relationships with musicians
    D   finding the time to visit music festivals

36 What does Jonny think has changed for guitar-makers in the UK?

    A   The training they receive is of a higher standard.
    B   A wider range of tools and equipment is available.
    C   Attitudes towards what makes a good guitar have moved on.
    D   Work methods have been introduced from America.

Part 6

You are going to read a newspaper article about the filming of a television documentary about icebergs. Six sentences have been removed from the article. Choose from the sentences **A–G** the one which fits each gap (**37–42**). There is one extra sentence which you do not need to use.

Mark your answers **on the separate answer sheet**.

Icebergs

There's more to icebergs than meets the eye – as I discovered filming on one of these gigantic Arctic fortresses as it slowly melted.

Imagine a solid sheet of frozen water 3 km across and 100 m thick. Imagine it floating quietly in dark ocean waters, somewhere between Canada and Greenland. Imagine the near-silent desolation of the inhospitable Arctic environment around it, getting harsher as winter approaches. **37** Imagine this forbidding, serene, massive place. But it really exists. This iceberg right now is floating in peace as we all go about our busy, bustling lives.

Back in the summer, things were different. This iceberg was a dynamic battleground, floodlit by 24-hour daylight. Once an iceberg is released from its parent glacier, its time is very limited. **38** Then mini-bergs break off the weakened front. Some of these events we witnessed were sudden, loud and violent. We had come to spectate on this oceanic siege, and to learn its rules.

The ice edge towered over us, vertical, angular and utterly spectacular. We steamed around the berg until we found lower cliffs, and suddenly the icescape behind was revealed. Gentle mounds are separated by valleys. **39** An iceberg makes its own fog, so we could only see a little way into the centre, peering hopefully over the top of the cliffs.

Curious polar bears peered back. We had thought we would be lucky to see one or two, but the iceberg turned out to have a healthy population of these huge carnivores. **40** They must wait for the sea ice to come back so that they can hunt. So they were snoozing away, not at all bothered that their chosen holiday home was moving, tilting, melting, breaking up and giving a TV production team and some scientists severe logistical headaches.

That's how I remember the iceberg, and that's the side of it you'll see if you watch the programmes. But since then things have changed. We left a GPS tracker as a passenger, so we know that the iceberg has travelled 60 miles, and is now about 30 miles south of where it was in August. Only 65% of it is left. The iceberg only gets 7 hours and 40 minutes of daylight now, and soon the darkness will swallow it up completely. **41** Winter is beginning, and with it returns a period of stability.

Sea ice is advancing towards the berg from the north. This is the other type of ice at the poles, formed when the sea surface itself freezes. In an average year, the sea ice would already have reached our iceberg. But this year, there was less summer sea ice in the Arctic than any other year on record, so it is taking longer for the great freeze to reach it. The sea ice is still crawling south. **42** Then the iceberg will be frozen in place. Darkness and silence will rule. The bears will be able to walk out on to the sea ice and hunt again.

A These lead down to waterfalls of meltwater cascading into the ocean.

B But it will lose the battle in the end and the last piece of solid ice will melt.

C When it touches the cliffs that I saw, it will connect our iceberg to all the other ice in the Arctic.

D The ice fights a losing battle along its edges, as warm ocean water eats into it.

E The only sound comes from water lapping against the ice, and a lone seal swimming nearby.

F The Arctic summer can, however, be a very hard time for them.

G The supply of energy from the sun is so weak, the battle is over for this year.

Part 7

You are going to read an article about a new exercise craze called *Zuu* and its inventor Nathan Helberg. For questions **43–52**, choose from sections (**A–E**). The sections may be chosen more than once.

Mark your answers **on the separate answer sheet**.

In which section does the writer

comment on how little rest she seems to be given after one exercise?	43	
become aware of the limitations of her usual fitness routine?	44	
say she hopes that the next exercise is not so demanding?	45	
mention a deal she did with Nathan that benefited them both?	46	
imply that a conventional keep-fit method is less natural than *Zuu*?	47	
compare the movements of *Zuu* with those of earlier humans?	48	
explain that she has chosen just one of the exercises to perform regularly?	49	
say how slow and awkward she feels doing a particular exercise?	50	
give examples of situations where lack of activity affects people's bodies?	51	
cast doubt on one of Nathan's ideas?	52	

Exercise like an animal

Journalist Annabel Venning tries a new exercise craze

A

Our sedentary lifestyles mean that most of us aren't using our muscles properly. As small children we squat, crawl and leap around freely, but the older we get the more restricted our movements become and many of our muscles get little action as we sit at desks or in cars. Occasionally we hit the gym, where we use machines to work on specific muscles rather than the whole body. Now a new form of fitness, an intense workout based on simple animal movements such as crawling, is taking off. Its Australian founder, Nathan Helberg, has been using it with the military, police forces, schoolchildren and even prisoners. He took his inspiration from martial arts, break-dancing, the animal world and the dance movements of indigenous people, and developed *Zuu*.

B

There are around 100 animal movements – although beginners start with 25 – that work muscles, joints and ligaments as well as improving heart and lung fitness. *Zuu* needs no equipment and little space. The idea is to train your body to do the kinds of activities that our ancestors had to do in daily life. It's quick, it tops up your strength and it's not aiming to give you big muscles. In exchange for the publicity from my article, Nathan offers me a master class, alongside two of his trainers, a privilege that would otherwise be beyond my financial means! I am daunted by the prospect of doing things I haven't done since my pre-school years.

C

We do each movement for 30 seconds (for my benefit – as you get fitter, you keep on for 45 seconds). We start with a frog squat: legs wide, knees bent, elbows locked inside knees. It's a little undignified, but fine at first. Then as

the seconds go by, the fronts of my thighs start to burn and it's all I can do not to collapse. After the 30 seconds we dash back across the room to our starting point with barely a moment to catch our breath. Nathan assures me the frog squat is particularly good for the lower backs of office workers, and recommends that they should take a break and perform the movement for four minutes a day. Somehow I can't see this working!

D

Then it's on to a bear crawl, on hands and feet. While Nathan and others shoot across the room, I lumber along like an ancient grizzly bear. Then we do it again – backwards. I seem to be clumsy, but it does get slightly easier as I go on. This movement evidently uses every joint in the body, strengthening things like ligaments and tendons, while at the same time raising heart rate as effectively as running. Perhaps being a snake will be easier. But there's no lying flat on our stomachs. Instead we have to raise our bodies 2 cm off the floor, rocking our weight back and forth from hands to toes. It's a bit of an effort to keep going for the full minute.

E

By the end I'm shaking with exhaustion. Despite my initial reservations, by the end of my session, I have started to enjoy myself. Mind you, it's hard not to laugh when you're imitating a bear on rewind! I thought I was in reasonably good shape – I run 5 km three times a week – but after this I realise how little I push myself normally. Nathan has promised that I could increase my upper body strength by 30% in just six weeks by doing classes. I have compromised and do bear crawls around my garden at home during work breaks, much to the amazement of my dog!

WRITING (1 hour 20 minutes)

Part 1

You **must** answer this question. Write your answer in **140–190** words in an appropriate style **on the separate answer sheet**.

---

1   In your English class you have been talking about self-employment. Now, your English teacher has asked you to write an essay.

Write your essay using **all** the notes and giving reasons for your point of view.

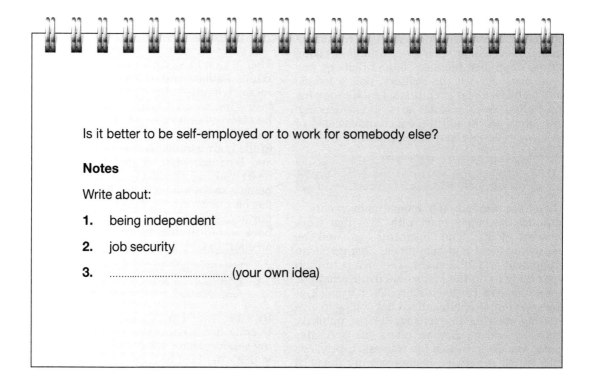

Is it better to be self-employed or to work for somebody else?

Notes

Write about:

1.   being independent

2.   job security

3.   .... (your own idea)

Part 2

Write an answer to **one** of the questions **2–4** in this part. Write your answer in **140–190** words in an appropriate style **on the separate answer sheet**. Put the question number in the box at the top of the answer sheet.

---

2   You have seen this notice in an online holiday magazine:

> *Reviews wanted*
>
> ## Sports Holidays
>
> We're looking for reviews of organised holidays where people can practise sports.
>
> Write a review of the holiday, including information about the place, the sports, and how well organised the holiday was.

Write your **review**.

3   You see this notice in an English-language magazine:

> *Articles wanted*
>
> ### Being famous for something
>
> If you could be famous for something, what would you like to be famous for? Why?
>
> The best articles will be printed next month.

Write your **article**.

4   You receive this email from your English-speaking friend, Nico:

> **Subject: Where to study?**
>
> Hi
> I'm going to university next year. I can either go to the university in my home town and live at home, or study in another area and live away from home.
> What do you think I should do?
> Write soon
> Nico

Write your **email**.

LISTENING (approximately 40 minutes)

Part 1

You will hear people talking in eight different situations.

For questions **1–8**, choose the best answer (**A**, **B** or **C**).

---

1 You hear a man talking about collecting old coins.

What pleases him most about his hobby?

    A the satisfaction of aiming for a complete collection

    B the idea that someone has used the coins in the past

    C the thrill of searching for unusual coins for his collection

2 You hear a woman talking about playing the piano.

What does she say about learning to play the piano?

    A It's important to find the right teacher.

    B Everyone can play well if they try.

    C It requires more discipline than other instruments.

3 You overhear a man and a woman talking in an art gallery about a boy's paintings.

What do they agree about the paintings?

    A They show remarkable artistic maturity.

    B The gallery is asking too much money for them.

    C They probably weren't painted by the boy.

4 You hear two students talking about a university chemistry lecturer.

What do they agree about the lecturer?

    A She is good at explaining difficult concepts in lectures.

    B She is tolerant towards students who hand work in late.

    C She manages to make students feel enthusiastic about her subject.

5   You hear a woman talking to a work colleague about moving abroad for a new job.

What does the woman feel disappointed about?

A   the inflexible attitude to the start date

B   the lack of job security involved

C   the relatively low status of the work

6   You hear two friends talking about a job interview.

How does the woman feel now?

A   surprised that the interview went well

B   pleased to have impressed the interviewers

C   relieved that she wasn't asked any difficult questions

7   You hear part of a radio programme.

What is the woman talking about?

A   an environment group

B   a nature course for school children

C   a new walking route in the countryside

8   You hear a woman talking to her brother about his hair.

What is she doing?

A   admitting she cut his hair badly

B   teasing him about his haircut

C   suggesting he grow his hair longer

Part 2

You will hear a man called David Briggs giving a talk about his work as a volunteer on a turtle conservation programme in Western Australia. For questions **9–18**, complete the sentences with a word or short phrase.

Working on a turtle conservation programme

David first found out about the turtle programme from his **(9)** ....

David chose to work at the **(10)** .... site because its location was more convenient.

David thinks his interest in **(11)** .... helped him to get a place on the programme.

David was surprised to find that the ability to **(12)** .... wasn't considered necessary.

Apart from the cost of **(13)** .... everything essential was provided by the organisers.

David's shifts took place during the **(14)** .... when the turtles could

be checked on the beach.

David felt it was particularly important to be **(15)** .... when handling the turtles.

Unlike his fellow volunteers, David found the **(16)** .... didn't bother him.

David said that tiredness could lead to a loss of **(17)** .... among the

volunteers when they were collecting data.

David uses the name **(18)** .... to refer to the most experienced volunteers.

Part 3

You will hear five short extracts in which writers give advice about writing comedy scripts for television. For questions **19–23**, choose which piece of advice (**A–H**) each speaker gives. Use the letters only once. There are three extra letters which you do not need to use.

A Write about people who amuse you.

B Team up with another writer.

Speaker 1	19

C Develop your characters well.

Speaker 2	20

D Rewrite your whole script several times.

Speaker 3	21

E Study comedy you like.

Speaker 4	22

F Listen to what other people say about your work.

Speaker 5	23

G Find your own way as a writer.

H Let the audience in on the joke quickly.

Part 4

You will hear an interview with a woman called Maya Gardi, whose daily life and business are based on waste-free principles. For questions **24–30**, choose the best answer (**A**, **B** or **C**).

24 What did Maya find most difficult when she started shopping in a waste-free way?

    A having to take more time over it

    B having to avoid things in plastic containers

    C having to remember to take her own bags

25 Maya decided to adopt a completely waste-free lifestyle when she

    A saw an article online about plastic rubbish.

    B noticed the bins outside her block of flats.

    C visited her local waste facitilty.

26 How did Maya's parents react to her decision to live waste-free?

    A They were worried that she would regret it.

    B They did not believe that she really meant it.

    C They did not think that she was likely to succeed.

27 How have Maya's cooking and eating habits changed?

    A She uses leftover food creatively.

    B She cooks more often for her friends.

    C She has developed her own cooking skills.

28 What does Maya say about socialising?

    A She sometimes has to forget her principles.

    B She doesn't worry about what people think of her.

    C She carefully chooses which events she attends.

29 What does Maya say about her new business?

    A She has an advantage when it comes to marketing.

    B Sales are increasing faster than expected.

    C She is expanding into a related sector.

30 How did Maya feel about the radio work she did recently?

    A nervous about taking part at the last minute

    B pleased to have the chance to explain her views

    C surprised that she was asked by a reporter

SPEAKING (14 minutes)

You take the Speaking test with another candidate (possibly two candidates), referred to here as your partner. There are two examiners. One will speak to you and your partner and the other will be listening. Both examiners will award marks.

Part 1 (2 minutes)

The examiner asks you and your partner questions about yourselves. You may be asked about things like 'your home town', 'your interests', 'your career plans', etc.

Part 2 (a one-minute 'long turn' for each candidate, plus a 30-second response from the second candidate)

The examiner gives you two photographs and asks you to talk about them for one minute. The examiner then asks your partner a question about your photographs and your partner responds briefly.

Then the examiner gives your partner two different photographs. Your partner talks about these photographs for one minute. This time the examiner asks you a question about your partner's photographs and you respond briefly.

Part 3 (4 minutes)

The examiner asks you and your partner to talk together. They give you a task to look at so you can think about and discuss an idea, giving reasons for your opinion. For example, you may be asked to think about some changes in the world, or about spending free time with your family. After you have discussed the task for about two minutes with your partner, the examiner will ask you a follow-up question, which you should discuss for a further minute.

Part 4 (4 minutes)

The examiner asks some further questions, which leads to a more general discussion of what you have talked about in Part 3. You may comment on your partner's answers if you wish.

Test 3

READING AND USE OF ENGLISH (1 hour 15 minutes)

Part 1

For questions **1–8**, read the text below and decide which answer (**A**, **B**, **C** or **D**) best fits each gap. There is an example at the beginning (**0**).

Mark your answers **on the separate answer sheet**.

Example:

0 **A** devised   **B** invented   **C** thought   **D** constructed

0	A	B	C	D
	▭	▬	▭	▭

Imaginary friends in early childhood

Many children have an imaginary friend – that is a friend they have **(0)** .... It was once thought that only children who had difficulty in **(1)** .... relationships with others had imaginary friends. In fact, having an imaginary friend is probably a common **(2)** .... of a normal childhood as many children with lots of real friends also have an imaginary friend. The imaginary friend may help some children **(3)** .... with emotional difficulties, but for many, having an imaginary friend is just fun.

Most children, it appears, realise that their imaginary friend is not real. If people **(4)** .... asking about an imaginary friend, children often say, 'You know, my friend isn't real – I **(5)** .... him up.'

There is no firm evidence to say that having an imaginary friend **(6)** .... us anything about what a child will be like in the future. One **(7)** .... of research, though, has **(8)** .... that adults who once had imaginary friends may be more creative than those who did not.

1   **A** forming   **B** creating   **C** gaining   **D** producing

2   **A** state   **B** aspect   **C** situation   **D** point

3   **A** handle   **B** accept   **C** support   **D** cope

4   **A** keep   **B** persist   **C** maintain   **D** stay

5   **A** got   **B** put   **C** made   **D** set

6   **A** reveals   **B** informs   **C** tells   **D** advises

7   **A** item   **B** section   **C** unit   **D** piece

8   **A** suggested   **B** displayed   **C** presented   **D** notified

Part 2

For questions **9–16**, read the text below and think of the word which best fits each gap. Use only **one** word in each gap. There is an example at the beginning (**0**).

Write your answers **IN CAPITAL LETTERS on the separate answer sheet**.

Example: | 0 | | B | E | E | N | | | | | | | | | | | | | | |

Collecting stamps

Ever since postage stamps were first issued, people have (**0**) .... collecting them. At (**9**) .... this was regarded as just a hobby for children. Many people, though, continue collecting stamps throughout the whole of (**10**) .... lives. Although stamp collecting is no (**11**) .... as widespread as it once was, it remains (**12**) .... of the most popular hobbies.

The collections people make vary. Some want to obtain every stamp ever issued by a particular country. Others, though, are more interested in the pictures on stamps and collect as (**13**) .... stamps as possible which have, for example, a picture of a bird or maybe of an aeroplane.

It is (**14**) .... doubt very satisfying for a collector to feel such a collection is complete. However, in many cases this never happens (**15**) .... new stamps are being issued (**16**) .... the time. This may seem frustrating but it means that people can carry on collecting for as long as their interest lasts.

Part 3

For questions **17–24**, read the text below. Use the word given in capitals at the end of some of the lines to form a word that fits in the gap **in the same line**. There is an example at the beginning (**0**).

Write your answers **IN CAPITAL LETTERS on the separate answer sheet**.

Example: | 0 | D | A | N | G | E | R | O | U | S | | | | | | | | | |

The transcontinental railway

Before 1869 the journey from the east coast to the west coast of
the United States took between four and six months, travelling
through difficult and **(0)** .... country by wagon. With the west   **DANGER**
coast becoming increasingly wealthy, it was obvious that a better
route was needed. In the 1850s **(17)** .... began about building a   **DISCUSS**
transcontinental railway line linking the west with the east.

Although there was much **(18)** .... about the best route, eventually   **AGREEMENT**
it was decided to build a line. It ran 3,069 kilometres in **(19)** .... **LONG**
from Sacramento in the west to a point where it would join **(20)** ....   **EXIST**
lines giving access to the east coast.

Once the line became operational in 1869, the journey could be
completed in less than a week. In **(21)** .... with the six hours that a   **COMPARE**
(22) .... from New York to San Francisco takes nowadays, this may   **FLY**
not seem particularly **(23)** ...., but building the transcontinental   **IMPRESS**
railway was a great technological **(24)** .... which helped to bring   **ACHIEVE**
unity to the country.

Part 4

For questions **25–30**, complete the second sentence so that it has a similar meaning to the first sentence, using the word given. **Do not change the word given**. You must use between **two** and **five** words, including the word given. Here is an example (**0**).

Example:

0   A very friendly taxi driver drove us into town.

DRIVEN

We ……………..…..……………..…………… a very friendly taxi driver.

The gap can be filled by the words 'were driven into town by', so you write:

Example:	**0**	*WERE DRIVEN INTO TOWN BY*

Write **only** the missing words **IN CAPITAL LETTERS on the separate answer sheet**.

---

25   There was nobody with my brother when the accident happened.

OWN

My brother …………………..……………………………… when the accident happened.

26   I read only the first three chapters of the book because it was so boring.

GAVE

I …………………..………………………………… the book after the first three chapters because it was so boring.

27   I found it difficult to get on with my work because it was so hot.

MADE

The heat …………………..……………………………… me to get on with my work.

28 Sigmund accidentally left the door unlocked over the weekend.

MEAN

Sigmund .... the door unlocked over the weekend.

29 Mr Bateman was wrong to say that John had lost my keys.

SHOULD

Mr Bateman .... that John had lost my keys.

30 The opening of the new restaurant has been postponed for two weeks.

BE

It .... the new restaurant opens.

Part 5

You are going to read an article about a race between two famous brothers. For questions **31–36**, choose the answer (**A**, **B**, **C** or **D**) which you think fits best according to the text.

Mark your answers **on the separate answer sheet**.

An unusual race

To raise money for charity, a newspaper and a TV company challenged brothers Jonny and Alistair Brownlee, champion triathletes, to take part in a unique race that would set man against car, and brother against brother. In the wild and mountainous Yorkshire Dales of northern England, Jonny and younger brother Alistair would race to the same point, Jonny in a car on roads, Alistair across country on a mountain bike.

'I'm looking forward to it,' Jonny said, as the brothers took their places on the start line. 'I've never done anything like this before: it's exciting! These roads have beautiful views – and also it's very cold at the moment, so I'll be able to sit in the car and stay nice and warm.' Alistair was similarly eager – though in contrast to Jonny's jeans and sweatshirt, he was decked out in full winter cycling gear. Not that the cold was denting his confidence. 'To be honest,' he said, 'I've seen his driving before, so I'm not sure he's even going to make it. I might just stop for a cup of tea halfway up.'

The race started at the beautiful Semerwater lake in Wensleydale and was to finish at Yorkshire's highest road, Fleet Moss, some 350 metres up. No problem for the car, perhaps – but with Alistair's first couple of miles involving a 25 per cent incline, the younger Brownlee brother had his work cut out from the start. Barely time for a quick handshake and they were off. As Alistair sprinted away on his bike, heading for a track going straight up the hill and then across country to Fleet Moss, Jonny jumped in the car and was soon on the road. The next time the brothers would see each other would be at the finish line.

Jonny's early confidence took an immediate blow. Barely 15 seconds into the drive and he faced his first obstacle. Lumbering out of a field and into the road was a giant tractor.

'Welcome to Yorkshire,' he complained to the cameraman in the back of his car. 'If Alistair beats me, it's all down to this farmer!' Tense moments later, the tractor safely dealt with, Jonny was back in control.

Alistair, meanwhile, was struggling with the slope. Barely a couple of miles in and, as his brother relaxed, he was forced to dismount and carry his bike up the hill, past walls and over fences. Bemused sheep gazed, as the *line 51* Olympic champion kept up a steady pace, at the bizarre sight of a man in a field with a bike on his shoulders. And then, finally, the summit was reached. Over the other side was open ground, and with the sun coming out and the land spread before him, a chance to show what he was made of. Head down, feet on the pedals, Alistair was picking up speed.

In the car, his brother faced another local obstacle. The villages in this part of Yorkshire have stood since well before the invention of the car – and the roads that link them were not exactly made for speed. Jonny attempted to negotiate another absurdly narrow corner. The car slowed to a crawl, then passed through a stream that had formed on the road.

Clear of the last village, the car was on a straight race to the finishing line. Neither brother knew how close the other was. As Jonny roared the engine and sped through the final straight to Fleet Moss, Alistair was flying across his last field and back onto the road himself – approaching the finish from the other side. Head down, legs pumping… and then a squeal of brakes as he reached the line. And then, finally, Alistair looked up. 'Is he here?' he asked the waiting crowd. 'No? Really?' The head went back, the arms up. 'Yes!' Minutes later, the car pulled up and Jonny stepped out. 'Well done,' Jonny said with disappointment. 'I'm gutted.'

31 The writer explains that before the race the brothers were alike in

    A being dressed for difficult conditions.
    B having plenty of enthusiasm for it.
    C feeling anxious about the weather.
    D believing in their own ability to win.

32 What is suggested about the start of the race?

    A The brothers appeared very uncertain of the route.
    B Alistair's training had been insufficient.
    C Jonny had a noticeable advantage.
    D The brothers tried to avoid eye contact with each other.

33 What is suggested about Alistair in the fifth paragraph?

    A He objected to the situation he found himself in.
    B He was relieved the hill was easier than expected.
    C He welcomed an opportunity to prove his ability.
    D He was distracted by the behaviour of some animals.

34 What does 'Bemused' mean in line 51?

    A annoyed
    B puzzled
    C distressed
    D disappointed

35 In the sixth paragraph, what do we learn about Jonny's progress?

    A He had to briefly break the speed limit.
    B He almost drove into some water.
    C He had to get the car through a tight space.
    D He nearly lost control of the car.

36 How did Alistair react when he reached the end of the race?

    A He worried his brother had got lost.
    B He celebrated by jumping off his bike.
    C He congratulated his brother on his performance.
    D He was uncertain who the winner was.

Part 6

You are going to read an article about a dam removal project. Six sentences have been removed from the article. Choose from the sentences **A–G** the one which fits each gap (**37–42**). There is one extra sentence which you do not need to use.

Mark your answers **on the separate answer sheet**.

Removing a dam to restore a river

Journalist Richard Lovett is taken to see how a river has come to life again after a dam has been removed.

Just outside the small town of Stabler in Washington, hydrologist Bengt Coffin surveys a mountain river he helped to revive. Today, the clear waters of Trout Creek run fast between banks covered in young alder trees. But just five years ago, an eight-metre-high concrete wall blocked the river at the site. This dam and the reservoir behind it had changed the river completely and made it difficult for fish such as the endangered steelhead trout to return to where they were born in order to breed. For one thing, the reservoir was full of sediment – mud, sand and gravel. It was Coffin who led the US Forest Service effort to remove the dam.

This is all part of a growing trend in the United States. An increasing number of dams are being removed, for financial and environmental reasons. **37** Some schemes take a slow path, restoring river flow over months or years. Others use explosives and other engineering techniques to drain reservoirs within hours.

At Trout Creek, Coffin and his colleagues decided to take the cautious route when removing the ageing Hemlock Dam. **38** The dam had been designed to include what is called a fish ladder, which allows fish and other animals to bypass the dam and swim upstream, but it was poorly built by modern standards and the number of fish using it had steadily declined.

A bigger concern was the reservoir, which had been steadily filling in with sediment. **39** Coffin holds a hand above his knee to make the point. In the midsummer sun, temperatures in the water could reach 26°C; 'Too warm for steelhead,' he says.

Coffin and others worried that flooding the river with all that sediment would harm the steelhead further downstream. The solution was to divert the river into a big pipe and then hire a fleet of dumper trucks to carry away all the sediment. **40** They then reinforced its banks with logs to stop them from eroding.

All those efforts seem to have worked. Just seven hours after water was allowed to flow back, Coffin's team could clearly see the first steelhead venturing into the new channel upstream from the old dam site. But there is another sign of success which Coffin is keen to reveal. **41** The rounded stones on it range from the size of potatoes to loaves of bread, and make walking difficult. But Coffin is thrilled to see them because they are newly arrived, having just been washed in by the current.

The stones in the river provide nesting spots for the steelhead and a habitat for the insects that they eat. **42** To illustrate this, he turns over a couple of rocks and points out six types of insect clinging to the underside, including caddisfly larvae and a stonefly. 'The year after the dam was removed, these wouldn't have been here,' he adds with satisfaction.

A The water there had become so shallow that it was possible for people to wade all the way across.

B 'People pay attention to the big fish,' Coffin says. 'Yes, they're an important part of the system, but they're not the only things.'

C One result of these projects has been an unanticipated research opportunity to study how to minimize the damage caused by releasing huge floods of water and decades of sediment.

D However, the reservoir lost its water and much of its mud, sand and gravel in three hours.

E Coffin leads me through patches of alder trees that were planted after the dam was removed, then crosses a rocky beach by the river.

F In the process of doing this, the workers rediscovered the river's original channel along the reservoir bottom.

G Built back in 1935, the structure provided power and irrigation for a nearby tree nursery that shut down in 1997.

Part 7

You are going to read an article in which four people talk about giving up successful careers to do something very different. For questions **43–52**, choose from the people (**A–D**). The people may be chosen more than once.

Mark your answers **on the separate answer sheet**.

___

Which person

is not always confident that they have done the right thing?	43
is pleased to have proved doubters wrong?	44
says they found success more easily in their first career than in their second?	45
regrets not having changed careers sooner?	46
refers to a time when they needed to gain confidence?	47
mentions a sense of amazement when looking back at the past?	48
admits that they changed career too suddenly?	49
describes an urge to return to a childhood interest?	50
says that skills developed in their first career proved useful?	51
mentions feeling envious at one point?	52

I gave up my career for something very different

A Mike Donne

I started doing magic tricks for family and friends when I was about seven, and by sixteen I was performing at big public events. I was also good academically, and studied law at university. Ten years after my degree, I was a busy lawyer with no time for magic, although I missed it. Then, out of the blue, a couple of old friends asked if I'd let them use some of my old material in a touring magic show they were setting up. I agreed but it bothered me that they were doing something I'd always loved, while I was in a job I had very little passion for. So, I joined them. I was very rusty initially, and I had to practise for several months before I felt able to perform in public, but I'm now one of the main acts. Funnily enough, it's been far tougher to make it as a magician than as a lawyer, but I've realised that this is what makes me feel alive.

B Kristina Mayer

I used to work for a bank and made enough from that to be in a position to buy my own apartment when I was 22. After a few years, however, dissatisfaction set in. I was just sitting at a computer, manipulating figures, and I longed to get out into the fresh air and move around. Then, one weekend, some friends talked me into going surfing with them. Surprisingly, it appealed to me so much that I ended up spending my days surfing and doing restaurant work in the evenings. I'm now taking part in competitions and I promote surf gear as a professional surfer. At times I can hardly afford to pay the rent, and I sometimes wonder whether leaving the bank was such a good idea, but then I remember I'm doing my favourite thing in the world.

C Carl Johnson

Five years ago I was an accountant, well-paid but feeling unfulfilled in my life. Then, my cousin asked if I'd help out at his burger restaurant one weekend when he was short of staff. I'd always liked burgers ever since I was small, but I was surprised at how much I enjoyed making them. Two weeks later I quit my job, hired a van and some equipment, and started selling burgers at street markets. It would've been better to have taken more time doing some proper background research, but what I knew about accounting came in handy, and my enthusiasm made up for my inexperience. I've now acquired a second van and taken on a couple of assistants, so the business is growing. It's incredible to think how much my life has changed.

D Agnes Porter

I was a very creative child, but I was taught that success lay in other directions. So I worked hard and ended up as human resources manager of an international company. It was well-paid but I dreamed of starting my own business. So during one holiday last year, I decided to experiment and made cakes for a couple of wedding receptions. They turned out to be very popular and, within a month, I'd resigned from my job and was making cakes full-time. Pushing myself hard to do well is in my nature, so I still work a lot, but I feel more in control of things now. People used to say that having my own business was an unrealistic dream, so demonstrating I could achieve it has been very satisfying. It's just a pity I didn't do it several years ago.

WRITING (1 hour 20 minutes)

Part 1

You **must** answer this question. Write your answer in **140–190** words in an appropriate style **on the separate answer sheet**.

---

1 In your English class you have been talking about advertising. Now, your English teacher has asked you to write an essay.

Write your essay using **all** the notes and giving reasons for your point of view.

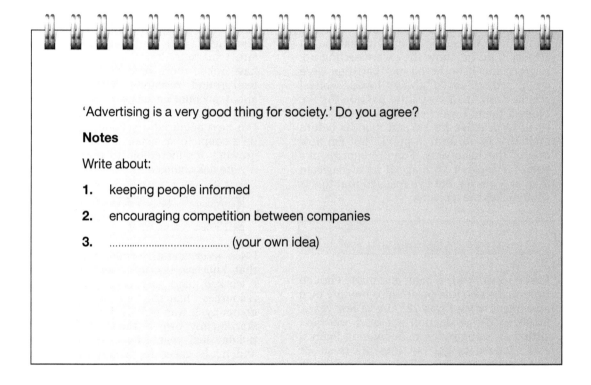

'Advertising is a very good thing for society.' Do you agree?

Notes

Write about:

1. keeping people informed

2. encouraging competition between companies

3. .... (your own idea)

Part 2

Write an answer to **one** of the questions **2–4** in this part. Write your answer in **140–190** words in an appropriate style **on the separate answer sheet**. Put the question number in the box at the top of the answer sheet.

2   You see this notice in an English-language magazine:

> *Articles wanted*
>
> # Changes!
>
> Some people love changes, others dislike them. What about you?
> Which changes in your life have had a big effect on you?
>
> The best articles will be printed next month.

Write your **article**.

3   This is an email you have received from your English-speaking friend, Marcus:

> **Subject: Learning English**
>
> Hi
> I'm researching the ways people learn English in different countries. Can you write and tell me about the most popular ways of learning English for people in your country?
> Write soon
> Marcus

Write your **email**.

4   You have seen this notice on a travel website:

> *Reviews wanted*
>
> ## Guidebooks for tourists
>
> We're looking for reviews of a good guidebook to your city or country.
>
> In your review you should include information about:
> - the contents of the book
> - what makes the book useful and interesting
> - why it's better than similar guidebooks.

Write your **review**.

LISTENING (approximately 40 minutes)

Part 1

You will hear people talking in eight different situations.

For questions **1–8**, choose the best answer (**A**, **B** or **C**).

---

1 You hear a young woman who is an apprentice cook talking about her apprenticeship.

How does she feel about it?

   A grateful to be working in a four-star restaurant

   B pleased that her teacher told her about the opportunity

   C confident about fulfilling her ambitions

2 You hear two students talking about passing the time on bus journeys.

What technique for passing the time do they both sometimes use?

   A listening to music

   B observing the world outside

   C concentrating on what's happening inside

3 You hear a cycle coach telling his group about the ride they are going to do.

What instruction does the coach give?

   A Don't go too fast on the return route.

   B Stick together on the main road.

   C Don't take the first sign to the destination.

4 You hear part of an interview in which a writer talks about autobiographies.

What does the writer say about them?

   A He prefers working on books about people he knows.

   B He is unlikely to write one himself.

   C He thinks the more popular ones are very boring.

5   You hear a journalist telling a colleague about her time at university.

How did she first get interested in journalism?

A by doing research online

B by accepting a chance request

C by reading a particularly interesting article

6   You hear a man and a woman talking about a new clothes shop they have visited.

What does the man say about having a member of staff to welcome customers?

A It seems like a worthwhile idea.

B Other people might appreciate it.

C Worse things happen in other shops.

7   You overhear a woman talking on the phone to a friend.

What is the woman talking about?

A an idea for a small short-term business

B the various career options open to her

C her role in a forthcoming expedition

8   You hear part of a broadcast on the radio.

What type of broadcast is it?

A a programme advertisement

B a wildlife documentary

C a news summary

Part 2

You will hear a woman called Paula Kanning, who works as a film advisor in local government, talking about her work. For questions **9–18**, complete the sentences with a word or short phrase.

Film Advisor

Paula's job title when she started working in the film department was **(9)** ....

Paula was first attracted to the job by the **(10)** .... on offer.

The most popular place for filmmakers in Paula's area is a **(11)** ....

Paula mentions a well-known advertisement for **(12)** .... that she proposed the site for.

Paula mentions that in her first year she sometimes needed to persuade

(13) .... to agree to filming.

Paula is particularly proud of the **(14)** .... she built up during her first

year in the department.

Paula's current job involves managing a project with the name **(15)** ....

Paula finds creating **(16)** .... for tourists the most difficult part of her current job.

Paula believes it is necessary to protect the **(17)** .... of local residents

as well as their property.

Paula's department has recently set up what she calls a **(18)** .... scheme for students.

Part 3

You will hear five short extracts in which people talk about why they did not go to university directly after leaving school. For questions **19–23**, choose which of the reasons (**A–H**) each speaker gives. Use the letters only once. There are three extra letters which you do not need to use.

A   a wish to see new places

B   a misunderstanding about applying

Speaker 1	19

C   a desire to have a break from studying

Speaker 2	20

D   a wish to stay near to home

Speaker 3	21

E   a decision to prioritise family commitments

F   a desire to start a career immediately

Speaker 4	22

G   a feeling of not being mature enough

Speaker 5	23

H   an inability to find a suitable course

Part 4

You will hear a radio interview with a woman called Susan Fletcher, who works on a research station in Antarctica. For questions **24–30**, choose the best answer (**A**, **B** or **C**).

24 How does Susan feel before each trip to Antarctica?

    A anxious because she'll miss people she cares about

    B concerned about dealing with what lies ahead

    C relieved to be leaving problems behind

25 Susan says that what's most stressful for her at the moment is

    A not being able to predict everything you may need.

    B not having enough time to prepare properly.

    C not knowing exactly where she's going.

26 What does Susan admire about her colleagues?

    A their scientific skills

    B their lack of selfishness

    C their success as researchers

27 Susan says the entertainment that's organised at the research station

    A serves a useful purpose.

    B allows people to show off their talents.

    C disturbs people's regular schedules.

28 On the research station, Susan sometimes has difficulty

    A getting enough time alone.

    B eating the same food all the time.

    C having a comfortable night's sleep.

29 What does Susan say she loves about her work?

    A the chance to observe such fascinating wildlife

    B being able to live so far from populated areas

    C the fact that such a unique place is so familiar to her

30 Susan advises students hoping to work in Antarctica to

    A make sure they have skills that are not purely academic.

    B develop a high level of competence in their particular subject.

    C think carefully about whether they're well-suited to the lifestyle.

SPEAKING (14 minutes)

You take the Speaking test with another candidate (possibly two candidates), referred to here as your partner. There are two examiners. One will speak to you and your partner and the other will be listening. Both examiners will award marks.

Part 1 (2 minutes)

The examiner asks you and your partner questions about yourselves. You may be asked about things like 'your home town', 'your interests', 'your career plans', etc.

Part 2 (a one-minute 'long turn' for each candidate, plus a 30-second response from the second candidate)

The examiner gives you two photographs and asks you to talk about them for one minute. The examiner then asks your partner a question about your photographs and your partner responds briefly.

Then the examiner gives your partner two different photographs. Your partner talks about these photographs for one minute. This time the examiner asks you a question about your partner's photographs and you respond briefly.

Part 3 (4 minutes)

The examiner asks you and your partner to talk together. They give you a task to look at so you can think about and discuss an idea, giving reasons for your opinion. For example, you may be asked to think about some changes in the world, or about spending free time with your family. After you have discussed the task for about two minutes with your partner, the examiner will ask you a follow-up question, which you should discuss for a further minute.

Part 4 (4 minutes)

The examiner asks some further questions, which leads to a more general discussion of what you have talked about in Part 3. You may comment on your partner's answers if you wish.

Test 4

READING AND USE OF ENGLISH (1 hour 15 minutes)

Part 1

For questions **1–8**, read the text below and decide which answer (**A**, **B**, **C** or **D**) best fits each gap. There is an example at the beginning (**0**).

Mark your answers **on the separate answer sheet**.

Example:

0   **A** points   **B** marks   **C** shows   **D** finds

0	A	B	C	D
	⬜	▬	⬜	⬜

An ancient cave interests scientists

At the base of a hill in South Africa, a cluster of huge stones **(0)** .... the entrance to one of humanity's oldest known dwelling places. In fact, humans have **(1)** .... Wonderwerk Cave for 2 million years – most recently in the early 1900s, when a farming family **(2)** .... it their home. Wonderwerk holds another distinction as well: the cave contains the earliest **(3)** .... evidence that our ancient ancestors were using fire for cooking.

Like many archaeological finds, this one was accidental. Researchers were trying to **(4)** .... the age of primitive stone tools that had been unearthed in the cave. In the process, they **(5)** .... across the ashes of a campfire containing what turned **(6)** .... to be remains of food from a million years ago. That was 200,000 years older than any **(7)** .... discovered remnants of human-controlled fire. At Wonderwerk, the researchers are digging ever deeper, analysing soil up to 1.8 million years old, **(8)** .... evidence of even older fires.

1   **A**   occupied   **B**   stayed   **C**   settled   **D**   remained

2   **A**   built   **B**   found   **C**   used   **D**   made

3   **A**   heavy   **B**   fixed   **C**   solid   **D**   dense

4   **A**   conclude   **B**   detect   **C**   notice   **D**   determine

5   **A**   came   **B**   looked   **C**   went   **D**   fell

6   **A**   out   **B**   in   **C**   off   **D**   back

7   **A**   last   **B**   previously   **C**   once   **D**   formerly

8   **A**   enquiring   **B**   looking   **C**   seeking   **D**   chasing

Part 2

For questions **9–16**, read the text below and think of the word which best fits each gap. Use only one word in each gap. There is an example at the beginning (**0**).

Write your answers **IN CAPITAL LETTERS on the separate answer sheet**.

Example: | **0** | *O* | *F* | | | | | | | | | | | | | | | | | | | |

The joys of horse riding

For me, riding a horse is a delightful combination **(0)** .... adventure, excitement and relaxation. You can proceed at a slow, peaceful trot **(9)** .... choose to go at full speed, **(10)** .... you prefer that. **(11)** .... I love most about being on a horse is that you get a different view of the world, seeing things you would not normally see, totally surrounded by nature. Each ride has **(12)** .... own appeal. I especially cherish cold, crisp days in winter when the ground sparkles with snow. Even riding in the rain has a certain appeal – splashing through puddles and galloping home quickly so **(13)** .... to escape the next downpour. **(14)** .... paths you ride along may be familiar, you can never quite predict the surprises beyond the next corner. Riding alone can be fabulous, but going out on horses with a friend is best of **(15)** .... Even the horses seem to enjoy the company of each **(16)** ....

Part 3

For questions **17–24**, read the text below. Use the word given in capitals at the end of some of the lines to form a word that fits in the gap **in the same line**. There is an example at the beginning (**0**).

Write your answers **IN CAPITAL LETTERS on the separate answer sheet**.

Example:

0	D	E	V	E	L	O	P	M	E	N	T							

Henry Ford

One of the most important contributions of the American businessman, Henry Ford to the **(0)** .... of the automobile was **DEVELOP**
as inventor of the moving assembly line in 1913. Before this, teams of factory workers would all work together to construct a complete car. With an assembly line, each **(17)** .... in **EMPLOY**
Ford's factory had a specific **(18)** .... for only one job when **RESPONSIBLE**
putting together the car. This **(19)** .... of labour resulted in **DIVIDE**
(20) .... cost savings and meant that the total time taken in **SIGNIFY**
producing the cars was shortened quite **(21)** .... With the addition **CONSIDER**
of an **(22)** .... system for moving the cars as they were being **INNOVATE**
assembled, Ford's factory turned out a finished car every 93 minutes.
Even then, cars were too **(23)** .... for most people. Therefore, Ford **COST**
raised the minimum wage for his factory workers which led to general
wage increases across America. In this way, cars became **(24)** .... **AFFORD**
for more people and therefore relatively inexpensive compared to
previous times.

Part 4

For questions **25–30**, complete the second sentence so that it has a similar meaning to the first sentence, using the word given. **Do not change the word given**. You must use between **two** and **five** words, including the word given. Here is an example (**0**).

Example:

0   A very friendly taxi driver drove us into town.

DRIVEN

We .... a very friendly taxi driver.

The gap can be filled by the words 'were driven into town by', so you write:

Example:	0	*WERE DRIVEN INTO TOWN BY*

Write **only** the missing words **IN CAPITAL LETTERS on the separate answer sheet**.

---

25   Thick fog prevented the plane from landing.

UNABLE

The plane .... of the thick fog.

26   Mr Brown was just about to leave home when he remembered he hadn't bought a ticket.

POINT

Mr Brown was .... home when he remembered he hadn't bought a ticket.

27   I first visited Rome ten years ago.

SINCE

It has .... first visit to Rome.

28 Helen didn't tell me anything about the interview she had yesterday.

WORD

Helen .... to me about the interview she had yesterday.

29 Membership of the club is open to anyone over eighteen.

AGE

Anyone who is more than eighteen .... a member of the club.

30 Carole is hardly ever late for work.

ALMOST

Carole is .... time for work.

Part 5

You are going to read an article by Cal Flynn, who went to the Arctic Circle to work for a company that runs husky sled trips. For questions **31–36**, choose the answer (**A**, **B**, **C** or **D**) which you think fits best according to the text.

Mark your answers **on the separate answer sheet**.

Working with huskies

Just over a year ago, I left my job to work with huskies in the Arctic Circle in the far north of Finland. At 26, I was restless. I was dreaming of Arctic landscapes, cold and bleak expanses, perhaps in reaction to the noise and crowded living of London. So I found a small company run by Anna McCormack, and her husband, Pasi Ikonen, deep in Finnish Lapland. They agreed to take me on as a husky dog handler for a busy winter season. From December to February, there is plenty of business taking tourists out on sled rides pulled by huskies across the ice and snow (for anything from an hour to a five-day stretch). They started with six dogs, which rapidly expanded to more than 100.

Recently, they took over a second property – the 'wilderness farm', which they wrote was a picturesque but basic outpost with untrustworthy electrics and no running water. I could join the team for three months, they told me, if I knew what I was letting myself in for. 'The hours are long, the conditions tough and the work very physical.' I started packing straight away.

November 6, London

On my flight out I look out of the window. It is said that spring marches north at a rate of about 26 km per day, a tidal wave of opening flowers and leaves. I think what I am seeing, however, is the opposite movement, with winter marching south, and the rivers freezing over.

November 7, Helsinki and Hetta

We drive north by bus through endless dark forest – thin conifers, weighed down by snow – stopping occasionally to let reindeer lumber out of the way. I arrive at the farm after dark, and am barely through the door when I'm handed a pair of boots and turned out into the

line 41 cold. 'Do you want to be thrown in at the deep end?' Anna asks. It's a rhetorical question.

I follow the sound of barking, which grows to a wall of noise by the time I reach the dogsheds. Three figures are running back and forth up the lines of huskies, pulling them out and harnessing them to sleds. The dogs are almost hysterical with excitement, straining against the ropes in their desperation to be off. I can barely hear to introduce myself, but the others are too harried to stop and talk much *line 51* anyway. I hover on the sidelines and rub the forehead of one of the quieter dogs. Someone gestures at me impatiently – 'Get in!' – and I almost fall into the nearest sled. A command rings out, and with a jerk we are off into the dark, with only a head torch for light.

November 15, Hetta

It does not take long to be initiated into the ranks of the husky guides. 'Are you useful?' Anna asks. I'm stumped. I don't know. Am I? Further questioning reveals that no, I am not: I have never driven a snowmobile, haven't done woodwork since school and have never chopped anything with an axe. 'You do have a driving licence?' someone asks finally. I nod, relieved.

The basics of dog-sledding can be picked up very quickly: lean into the corners, put both feet on the brake to stop, and, whatever happens, don't let go of the handlebar. But everything else seems to be very complicated. Simple tasks such as feeding and watering the dogs become very difficult in sub-zero conditions. A bowl of water will freeze solid while you watch, so we must make a 'soup' of meat in hot water for the dogs. By the end of my first week my head is going round and round after so many instructions and my muscles ache from dragging heavy sleds – and from being dragged around myself by overenthusiastic huskies. But I am triumphant. 'I can chop with an axe, hammer a nail, and use a circular saw,' I email friends excitedly. 'In the snow.'

31 What were Cal's feelings when leaving London?

    A   convinced she needed to be somewhere more relaxing
    B   happy to further her knowledge of the tourism industry
    C   looking forward to helping Anna and Pasi build their business
    D   longing for a contrast to her current lifestyle

32 What was Cal's reaction to the description of the farm?

    A   put off by its remoteness
    B   enthusiastic about taking on its challenges
    C   hopeful of extending her stay
    D   attracted to the idea of being part of a group

33 Cal uses the phrase 'thrown in at the deep end' in line 41 to indicate that she was

    A   pushed into thick layers of snow.
    B   expected to swim in deep icy water.
    C   given something demanding to do initially.
    D   asked to do more work than others.

34 What does 'harried' mean in line 51?

    A   pressured
    B   exhausted
    C   silenced
    D   irritated

35 What impression is given of life with the husky guides?

    A   There is a welcoming atmosphere.
    B   There is an unnecessary level of aggression.
    C   People focus on getting the job done.
    D   People are expected to wait around without complaining.

36 How does Cal describe her situation after a week?

    A   She finds certain tasks easier than she'd been told they would be.
    B   She is resentful of the curiosity shown by others about her character.
    C   She feels confused by all the things she has been told to do.
    D   She is dissatisfied with her achievements.

Part 6

You are going to read an article about a charitable project that feeds a million school children. Six sentences have been removed from the article. Choose from the sentences **A–G** the one which fits each gap (**37–42**). There is one extra sentence which you do not need to use.

Mark your answers **on the separate answer sheet**.

The man who organised meals for children all over the world from his garden shed

In a remote Scottish valley stands a small iron shed that is affecting the lives of a million children thousands of kilometres away. The shed was the birthplace in 2002 of a tiny charity called Mary's Meals, run by a man called Magnus MacFarlane-Barrow. Magnus now employs fifty people in the Scottish city of Glasgow, but continues to work from the shed himself.

Magnus used to work for a large humanitarian organisation, and this job took him all over the world. During one trip in 2002, he was being shown round a school by a local teacher, when he asked a young boy of 14 what his dreams were. The boy said, 'to have enough food to eat and to go to school.' **37** He would provide dinner for them each day they were at school.

As he researched it over a lengthy period, Magnus found that many children around the world were going to school without having had any breakfast, 'and they weren't getting anything at school – so it would be evening before they got fed,' Magnus says. **38**

At the last count, Mary's Meals was working in 1,300 schools in 12 countries across four continents, providing school meals to 996,926 children each day. 'You find that when school dinners are provided, enrolment increases by around 18% – in some instances it's a lot more and the school roll has doubled in a matter of weeks,' says Magnus. **39** 'And attendance rates go up too, because in many schools children are enrolled but don't attend school very often, and that changes once they know they will be fed. And academic performance also improves a lot – because now not only are children coming in to school, they are also not hungry in lessons.'

The successes are all the more remarkable given the fact that it costs relatively little to feed a child for a whole school year. While Mary's Meals has grown dramatically, it has a modest income in comparison with other charities. **40** The school feeding programmes are run by local communities. Mary's Meals works to establish links with local farmers and community leaders such as teachers. These people organise a small army of volunteers, most of them mothers, who cook and serve the meals. Mary's Meals provides the kitchen, with all the cooking equipment. It also pays for the locally sourced food and gives training.

In 2012 one young supporter of Mary's Meals, nine-year-old Martha Payne, catapulted the charity to new heights of fame when she started a fundraising blog about her own unhealthy school dinners in Scotland and was briefly banned from doing so by her local council. **41** The decision was soon reversed after protests on the internet.

Magnus's main focus, however, remains more global. **42** There are, he says, an enormous number of children across the world who are not in school because of hunger and poverty. 'In many ways, I feel we are just beginning.'

A <u>This</u> was an idea of brilliant simplicity, but proved complex to put into practice.

B The sums involved are still enough to have a significant impact, though.

C <u>He</u> felt that was an intolerable <u>situation</u> and knew that changing it would make a big difference.

D The <u>incident</u> attracted a lot of attention, which <u>Magnus</u> admits was not unwelcome.

E Magnus realised <u>there</u> and then that there was one relatively simple intervention that could transform life for children all over the developing world.

F He is delighted with the way <u>things</u> have gone so far, but says there's a great deal that remains to be done.

G 'In the short term <u>that</u> can be problematic, but in the long term <u>it's fantastic</u>,' he adds.

Part 7

You are going to read a magazine article about being a journalist. For questions **43–52**, choose from the sections (**A–D**). The sections may be chosen more than once.

Mark your answers **on the separate answer sheet**.

In which section does the writer mention

having to rely on others when researching a story?	**43**	
how inspiration for articles can come from listening to people's conversations?	**44**	
some views on the state of the profession?	**45**	
the need to have realistic expectations?	**46**	
the pressure of having to meet deadlines?	**47**	
the importance of analysing what makes a good article?	**48**	
getting a sense of satisfaction from the responses of readers?	**49**	
the advantages of establishing positive relationships with other journalists?	**50**	
variety being a benefit of working as a journalist?	**51**	
the degree of preparation involved in producing different articles?	**52**	

So you want to become a journalist?

Susannah Butter tells us what being a journalist is really like.

A

A journalist's life can be hectic. The morning is usually the busiest part of the day because the newspaper I work on has to be ready for printing by noon. I work on the features pages – that is, on longer articles, often about interesting people's lives, which requires a lot of thought and organisation. With some of our articles we can take time to think, do proper research and write them in advance. Whereas others are more urgent, timely pieces with a quick turnaround. I'm sometimes asked to write a story that's needed for the next day. It can be scary knowing you have to find lots of information, write around 1,000 words and get ideas for pictures in just a few hours. I like digging up stuff that hasn't been reported and then presenting it in a way that readers will understand and value. It's great when you see people reading and enjoying a piece you've written. At all times, you need to think about how a story can be sold – for example, what accompanying picture and headline will draw people in.

B

Writing an article can involve having to find people's addresses and knocking on doors to ask them questions. My job allows me to meet and talk to a huge range of interesting people, and it changes all the time. In just one week, I might be working on an interview with a singer, a piece about coffee shops and an investigation into an unsolved crime. I think I'd get bored working on one thing all the time! My least favourite thing is probably chasing people for answers – this can involve a long chain of people that eventually leads you to the one person you want to write about. You have to be patient and persistent, politely reminding people what you want and when. You have to know just how far you can push them.

C

Pursuing a career in journalism was a natural choice for me because I'd always read newspapers and been quite nosy about other people's lives. At university, I did a bit of student journalism, editing the arts pages of a student newspaper and doing some writing. In my final year, I went to a careers talk about journalism. After I graduated, I emailed the journalist I'd met at the talk and asked her for work experience. I got it and really enjoyed it. People kept telling me that print journalism was dead, that there's no money in it in the age of the internet. But I figured that I'd give it a go anyway. I decided to take it seriously and get as qualified as I could. I've never regretted it.

D

For those considering a career in journalism, I would recommend reading as much as you can and keeping your eyes and ears open in everyday situations, which is great for getting ideas for stories. You also need to think about articles which work well and why, and remember this when you sit down to write your own. Being a good writer is an advantage, but in my experience journalism is as much about having new ideas and getting things done (preferably quickly!). But don't assume you will be writing front-page stories, or even having your name on any articles at first. Initially, it's about getting to know the people and the system. If they like you, they're more likely to give you an interesting task, listen to your ideas or give you advice.

WRITING (1 hour 20 minutes)

Part 1

You **must** answer this question. Write your answer in **140–190** words in an appropriate style **on the separate answer sheet**.

---

1   In your English class you have been talking about long-lasting products. Now, your English teacher has asked you to write an essay.

Write your essay using **all** the notes and giving reasons for your point of view.

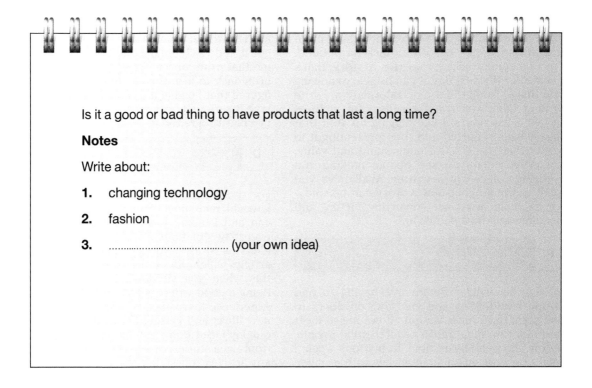

Is it a good or bad thing to have products that last a long time?

Notes

Write about:

1. changing technology

2. fashion

3. .... (your own idea)

Part 2

Write an answer to **one** of the questions **2–4** in this part. Write your answer in **140–190** words in an appropriate style **on the separate answer sheet**. Put the question number in the box at the top of the answer sheet.

---

2 In your English class you have been discussing the leisure activities, for example sports and clubs, available at your college. Your English teacher has now asked you to write a report.

In your report, you should:
- describe the current leisure facilities and activities in your college
- explain what improvements you would like to see
- say why these improvements would be popular with students.

Write your **report**.

3 You have seen this notice in an English online magazine:

Reviews wanted

Interesting Exhibitions

Have you been to an interesting exhibition recently? It could have been about art, photography, science or another subject. Write us a review:

- describing the exhibition
- explaining why you found it interesting
- saying which people you would recommend it to.

The best reviews will appear on the website.

Write your **review**.

4 You see this advertisement in a travel magazine:

Wanted: Walking guides

We are looking for people to take tourist groups walking in your area. You should:

- have a broad knowledge of the countryside in your area
- have experience of walking 15+ kms a day
- be a good communicator in English.

To apply, write to the project organiser, Ms Sally Morley, explaining why you are suitable for the job.

Write your **letter of application**.

LISTENING (approximately 40 minutes)

Part 1

You will hear people talking in eight different situations.

For questions **1–8**, choose the best answer (**A**, **B** or **C**).

---

1   You hear a man talking about an ancient object he found in the ground.

   The man took the object to a museum because

   A   he thought it might be valuable.

   B   he decided to record his find.

   C   he wanted to know what it was.

2   You hear two friends talking about advertising.

   What does the woman say about advertisements?

   A   They are merely a form of entertainment.

   B   They make people buy things they don't need.

   C   They give people misleading information about new products.

3   You hear an actor talking about her career.

   What does she say about how she became an actor?

   A   She had a chance meeting with someone.

   B   She was successful at drama school.

   C   She asked her friend to help her.

4   You hear a tour guide telling a group of tourists about a view.

   Which feature does the guide think will be most familiar to them?

   A   the park

   B   the river

   C   the wood

5   You hear a man talking to a friend about a presentation he has just given.

How does he feel now?

A   relieved that the audience was small

B   confident that he spoke clearly

C   surprised that so many people asked questions

6   You hear two students talking about a careers talk they have just heard at college.

What do they disagree about?

A   how useful the information was

B   how entertaining the speaker was

C   how well the audience behaved

7   You hear an author of children's books talking about her work.

What point is she making?

A   She wants her books to be educational.

B   Her books are about her real-life experiences.

C   Friendship is the main focus of her stories.

8   You hear a man and a woman talking about older people learning languages.

What does the man say about them?

A   They don't take advantage of technology.

B   They have more time to study.

C   They use better learning techniques.

Part 2

You will hear a student called Andy Richards talking about his recent trip to the tea growing region of Assam in Northern India. For questions **9–18**, complete the sentences with a word or short phrase.

Visit to a tea plantation

As part of his **(9)** .... course at university, Andy went to India to

gather information for a project.

Andy compares the tea plant's growing conditions to a **(10)** ....

Andy's group were invited to the **(11)** .... for the tea tasting session.

Andy was surprised that, as well as the leaves, the tea pickers also picked the

(12) .... of the plants.

On the elephant ride, Andy was able to see the **(13)** .... in the distance.

At the tea party, the **(14)** .... particularly impressed Andy.

When going over a **(15)** .... , Andy nearly fell off his motorbike.

In the market, Andy was very surprised to see the **(16)** .... on sale.

Andy was pleased with the price he paid for the **(17)** .... for his sister.

The **(18)** .... were Andy's favourite vegetables out of all those on

display at the market.

Part 3

You will hear five short extracts in which people are talking about work they did in shops. For questions **19–23**, choose from the options (**A–H**) what each person says about their experience. Use the letters only once. There are three extra letters which you do not need to use.

A My confidence was sometimes affected by customers' attitudes.

B I was pleased to discover that I had a good way with customers.

Speaker 1 [ ] **19**

C It made me appreciate the people I worked with.

Speaker 2 [ ] **20**

D The training I received didn't equip me to do my job well.

Speaker 3 [ ] **21**

E Customers were satisfied when they got a bargain.

Speaker 4 [ ] **22**

F I wasn't happy with some of the products in the shop.

Speaker 5 [ ] **23**

G It was motivating to sell more than the other assistants.

H It exhausted me both physically and mentally.

Part 4

You will hear an interview with Marvin Benby, a beekeeper who keeps his bees in hives on a city rooftop. For questions **24–30**, choose the best answer (**A**, **B** or **C**).

24 What made Marvin get into beekeeping?

  A He was persuaded to try it by a friend.

  B A friend offered to teach him about it.

  C He wanted to prove a friend wrong.

25 Marvin thinks the best part about keeping bees is

  A helping to increase the bee population.

  B the excitement of checking his beehives.

  C having access to so much honey.

26 One of the difficulties for Marvin of city beekeeping is

  A taking it personally when things go wrong.

  B ensuring the bees get to a variety of flowers.

  C getting hold of the most suitable equipment.

27 Marvin says that one of his neighbours

  A complained about being stung by a bee.

  B insisted that Marvin moved his beehives.

  C had concerns due to an allergy to bees.

28 When Marvin set up his first beehive

  A he became confused about what to do.

  B he made some potentially dangerous mistakes.

  C his bees became nervous and stressed.

29 What does Marvin say about selling bee-related products?

    A He has started to make a profit.

    B Local people are starting to buy them.

    C It cost him a lot to get started.

30 How does Marvin feel about the next few months?

    A He has a mixture of contrasting feelings.

    B He hopes to enjoy a more relaxed period.

    C He is confident that he can manage.

SPEAKING (14 minutes)

You take the Speaking test with another candidate (possibly two candidates), referred to here as your partner. There are two examiners. One will speak to you and your partner and the other will be listening. Both examiners will award marks.

Part 1 (2 minutes)

The examiner asks you and your partner questions about yourselves. You may be asked about things like 'your home town', 'your interests', 'your career plans', etc.

Part 2 (a one-minute 'long turn' for each candidate, plus a 30-second response from the second candidate)

The examiner gives you two photographs and asks you to talk about them for one minute. The examiner then asks your partner a question about your photographs and your partner responds briefly.

Then the examiner gives your partner two different photographs. Your partner talks about these photographs for one minute. This time the examiner asks you a question about your partner's photographs and you respond briefly.

Part 3 (4 minutes)

The examiner asks you and your partner to talk together. They give you a task to look at so you can think about and discuss an idea, giving reasons for your opinion. For example, you may be asked to think about some changes in the world, or about spending free time with your family. After you have discussed the task for about two minutes with your partner, the examiner will ask you a follow-up question, which you should discuss for a further minute.

Part 4 (4 minutes)

The examiner asks some further questions, which leads to a more general discussion of what you have talked about in Part 3. You may comment on your partner's answers if you wish.

Frames for the Speaking test

Test 1

Note: In the examination, there will be both an assessor and an interlocutor in the room.
  The visual material for **Test 1** appears on pages C1 and C2 (Part 2), and C3 (Part 3).

Part 1   2 minutes (3 minutes for groups of three)

Interlocutor: Good morning/afternoon/evening. My name is .... and this
                is my colleague ....
                And your names are?
                Can I have your mark sheets, please?
                Thank you.

- Where are you from, *(Candidate A)*?
- And you, *(Candidate B)*?

First, we'd like to know something about you.

*Select one or more questions from any of the following categories,
as appropriate.*

Family and friends
- Who are you most like in your family? (In what ways are you similar?)
- Do you go on holiday with your family? (Why? / Why not?)
- Have you done anything interesting with your friends recently?
  (What did you do with them?)
- Tell me about a really good friend of yours. (Do you share the same
  interests?)

Your interests
- Is there a sport or hobby you enjoy doing? (What do you do?)
  (Why do you like it?)
- If you could learn a new skill, what would you choose to do? (Why?)
- Do you like reading? (What do you read?) (Why do you like it?)
- Have you seen a good film recently? (Tell me about it.)

Future plans
- Have you got any plans for this weekend? (What are you going to do?)
- Are you going to go on holiday this year? (Where are you going to go?)
- Is there anything you'd like to study in the future? (Why?)
- Which country would you most like to visit in the future?
  (Do you think you'll go there one day?) (Why? / Why not?)

Part 2   4 minutes (6 minutes for groups of three)

Getting information
Walking

Interlocutor:	In this part of the test, I'm going to give each of you two photographs. I'd like you to talk about your photographs on your own for about a minute, and also to answer a question about your partner's photographs.
	(Candidate A), it's your turn first. Here are your photographs. They show people getting information about different things.
	Indicate the pictures on page C1 to the candidates.
	I'd like you to compare the photographs, and say why you think the people are getting information about these things.
	All right?
Candidate A:	*[1 minute.]*
Interlocutor:	Thank you.
	(Candidate B), do you enjoy travelling by plane? ...... (Why? / Why not?)
Candidate B:	*[Approximately 30 seconds.]*
Interlocutor:	Thank you.
	Now, *(Candidate B)*, here are your photographs. They show people walking in different places.
	Indicate the pictures on page C2 to the candidates.
	I'd like you to compare the photographs, and say why you think the people have decided to go walking in these places.
	All right?
Candidate B:	*[1 minute.]*
Interlocutor:	Thank you.
	(Candidate A), which of these places would you prefer to walk in? ...... (Why?)
Candidate A:	*[Approximately 30 seconds.]*
Interlocutor:	Thank you.

Parts 3 and 4   8 minutes (11 minutes for groups of three)

Part 3

Reading books

Interlocutor:	Now, I'd like you to talk about something together for about two minutes *(3 minutes for groups of three)*.
	Some people think that everyone should spend more of their free time reading books, and other people disagree. Here are some things they think about and a question for you to discuss. First you have some time to look at the task.
	Indicate the text on page C3 to the candidates. Allow 15 seconds.
	Now, talk to each other about whether everyone should spend more of their free time reading books.
Candidates:	*[2 minutes (3 minutes for groups of three).]*
Interlocutor:	Thank you. Now you have about a minute to decide what you think is the best reason for people to spend more of their free time reading books.
Candidates:	*[1 minute (for pairs and groups of three).]*
Interlocutor:	Thank you.

Part 4

Interlocutor: *Use the following questions, in order, as appropriate:*

- Some people say that students spend too much time at school reading, so they should do something different in their free time. Do you agree? (Why? / Why not?)

> *Select any of the following prompts, as appropriate:*
> - What do you think?
> - Do you agree?
> - And you?

- Some people say that we can't learn anything useful from reading novels. Do you agree? (Why? / Why not?)

- Do you think it's important for parents to read to their children? (Why? / Why not?)

- Do you think it's true that if we want to understand something well we should watch a TV documentary rather than read a book? (Why? / Why not?)

- Some people say that we don't need libraries any more. Do you agree? (Why? / Why not?)

- Do you think that in the future people won't read books at all? (Why? / Why not?)

Thank you. That is the end of the test.

Test 2

Note: In the examination, there will be both an assessor and an interlocutor in the room.
  The visual material for **Test 2** appears on pages C4 and C5 (Part 2), and C6 (Part 3).

Part 1   2 minutes (3 minutes for groups of three)

Interlocutor:	Good morning/afternoon/evening. My name is .... and this is my colleague .... And your names are? Can I have your mark sheets, please? Thank you.

- Where are you from, *(Candidate A)*?
- And you, *(Candidate B)*?

First, we'd like to know something about you.

Select one or more questions from any of the following categories, as appropriate.

Family and friends
- Who are you most like in your family? (In what ways are you similar?)
- Do you go on holiday with your family? (Why? / Why not?)
- Have you done anything interesting with your friends recently? (What did you do with them?)
- Tell me about a really good friend of yours. (Do you share the same interests?)

Your interests
- Is there a sport or hobby you enjoy doing? (What do you do?) (Why do you like it?)
- If you could learn a new skill, what would you choose to do? (Why?)
- Do you like reading? (What do you read?) (Why do you like it?)
- Have you seen a good film recently? (Tell me about it.)

Future plans
- Have you got any plans for this weekend? (What are you going to do?)
- Are you going to go on holiday this year? (Where are you going to go?)
- Is there anything you'd like to study in the future? (Why?)
- Which country would you most like to visit in the future? (Do you think you'll go there one day?) (Why? / Why not?)

Part 2   4 minutes (6 minutes for groups of three)

Holidays in different places
Choosing things

Interlocutor:	In this part of the test, I'm going to give each of you two photographs. I'd like you to talk about your photographs on your own for about a minute, and also to answer a question about your partner's photographs.
	(Candidate A), it's your turn first. Here are your photographs. They show people spending their holidays in different ways.
	Indicate the pictures on page C4 to the candidates.
	I'd like you to compare the photographs, and say what you think the people are enjoying about spending their holidays in these ways.
	All right?
Candidate A:	*[1 minute.]*
Interlocutor:	Thank you.
	(Candidate B), which of these things would you prefer to do? ...... (Why? / Why not?)
Candidate B:	*[Approximately 30 seconds.]*
Interlocutor:	Thank you.
	Now, *(Candidate B)*, here are your photographs. They show people choosing things in different situations.
	Indicate the pictures on page C5 to the candidates.
	I'd like you to compare the photographs, and say what the people might find difficult about choosing things in these situations.
	All right?
Candidate B:	*[1 minute.]*
Interlocutor:	Thank you.
	(Candidate A), do you often go shopping in supermarkets? ...... (Why? / Why not?)
Candidate A:	*[Approximately 30 seconds.]*
Interlocutor:	Thank you.

Parts 3 and 4   8 minutes (11 minutes for groups of three)

Part 3

Independent learning

Interlocutor:	Now, I'd like you to talk about something together for about two minutes *(3 minutes for groups of three)*.
	Some people think that it's a good idea to try and learn some things without a teacher, but other people disagree. Here are some things they think about and a question for you to discuss. First you have some time to look at the task.
	Indicate the text on page C6 to the candidates. Allow 15 seconds.
	Now, talk to each other about whether it's a good idea to try and learn some things without a teacher.
Candidates:	*[2 minutes (3 minutes for groups of three).]*
Interlocutor:	Thank you. Now you have about a minute to decide what you think is the best reason for learning new things with a teacher.
Candidates:	*[1 minute (for pairs and groups of three).]*
Interlocutor:	Thank you.

Part 4

Interlocutor:	*Use the following questions, in order, as appropriate:*

- Do you find it always better to have a teacher when you want to learn things? (Why? / Why not?)

- Some people say that we should keep learning new things all our lives. What do you think?

> *Select any of the following prompts, as appropriate:*
> - What do you think?
> - Do you agree?
> - And you?

- Do you think it's true that having a private lesson is better than having a lesson with other students? (Why? / Why not?)

- Do you think that in future everyone will learn everything they need to know from the internet? (Why? / Why not?)

- Some people say that out parents teach us more important things than any teachers. Do you agree? (Why? / Why not?)

- Some people say the only way we really learn things is by trying to do things and making mistakes. (What do you think?)

Thank you. That is the end of the test.

Test 3

Note: In the examination, there will be both an assessor and an interlocutor in the room.
  The visual material for **Test 3** appears on pages C7 and C8 (Part 2), and C9 (Part 3).

Part 1   2 minutes (3 minutes for groups of three)

Interlocutor: Good morning/afternoon/evening. My name is ………… and
                     this is my colleague …………. .
                     And your names are?
                     Can I have your mark sheets, please?
                     Thank you.

   • Where are you from, *(Candidate A)*?
   • And you, *(Candidate B)*?

First, we'd like to know something about you.

*Select one or more questions from any of the following categories,
as appropriate.*

Family and friends
• Who are you most like in your family? (In what ways are you similar?)
• Do you go on holiday with your family? (Why? / Why not?)
• Have you done anything interesting with your friends recently?
  (What did you do with them?)
• Tell me about a really good friend of yours. (Do you share the same
  interests?)

Your interests
• Is there a sport or hobby you enjoy doing? (What do you do?)
  (Why do you like it?)
• If you could learn a new skill, what would you choose to do? (Why?)
• Do you like reading? (What do you read?) (Why do you like it?)
• Have you seen a good film recently? (Tell me about it.)

Future plans
• Have you got any plans for this weekend? (What are you going to do?)
• Are you going to go on holiday this year? (Where are you going to go?)
• Is there anything you'd like to study in the future? (Why?)
• Which country would you most like to visit in the future?
  (Do you think you'll go there one day?) (Why? / Why not?)

Part 2   4 minutes (6 minutes for groups of three)

People using phones
Winter activities

Interlocutor:	In this part of the test, I'm going to give each of you two photographs. I'd like you to talk about your photographs on your own for about a minute, and also to answer a question about your partner's photographs.
	(Candidate A), it's your turn first. Here are your photographs. They show people using their phones in different situations.
	Indicate the pictures on page C7 to the candidates.
	I'd like you to compare the photographs, and say why you think the people have decided to use their phones in these situations.
	All right?
Candidate A:	*[1 minute.]*
Interlocutor:	Thank you.
	(Candidate B), do you often use a mobile phone? ...... (Why? / Why not?)
Candidate B:	*[Approximately 30 seconds.]*
Interlocutor:	Thank you.
	Now, (Candidate B), here are your photographs. They show people doing different activities in winter.
	Indicate the pictures on page C8 to the candidates.
	I'd like you to compare the photographs, and say what you think the people are enjoying about doing these winter activities.
	All right?
Candidate B:	*[1 minute.]*
Interlocutor:	Thank you.
	(Candidate A), which of these things would you prefer to do? ...... (Why? / Why not?)
Candidate A:	*[Approximately 30 seconds.]*
Interlocutor:	Thank you.

Parts 3 and 4   8 minutes (11 minutes for groups of three)

Part 3

University

Interlocutor:	Now, I'd like you to talk about something together for about two minutes *(3 minutes for groups of three)*.
	Some people think that students should go on to further education after they leave school. Here are some things they think about and a question for you to discuss. First you have some time to look at the task.
	Indicate the text on page C9 to the candidates. Allow 15 seconds.
	Now, talk to each other about whether students should go on to further education after they leave school.
Candidates:	*[2 minutes (3 minutes for groups of three).]*
Interlocutor:	Thank you. Now you have about a minute to decide what you think is the best reason for someone to go on to further education.
Candidates:	*[1 minute (for pairs and groups of three).]*
Interlocutor:	Thank you.

Part 4

Interlocutor:	*Use the following questions, in order, as appropriate:*

- Do a lot of students go on to university in your country? Do you think that's a good thing? (Why? / Why not?)

- Do you think it's a good idea for students to leave home and study in a different city after they finish school? (Why? / Why not?)

> *Select any of the following prompts, as appropriate:*
> - What do you think?
> - Do you agree?
> - And you?

- Is it a good idea to study in another country? (Why? / Why not?)

- Some people say that these days you need to have lots of qualifications to be successful. Do you agree? (Why? / Why not?)

- Some people say that further education doesn't prepare people for getting a job. Do you agree? (Why? / Why not?)

- Should students get some work experience while they're still at school or college? (Why? / Why not?)

Thank you. That is the end of the test.

Test 4

Note: In the examination, there will be both an assessor and an interlocutor in the room.
The visual material for **Test 4** appears on pages C10 and C11 (Part 2), and C12 (Part 3).

Part 1   2 minutes (3 minutes for groups of three)

Interlocutor:	Good morning/afternoon/evening. My name is .... and this is my colleague .... And your names are? Can I have your mark sheets, please? Thank you.

- Where are you from, *(Candidate A)*?
- And you, *(Candidate B)*?

First, we'd like to know something about you.

Select one or more questions from any of the following categories, as appropriate.

Family and friends
- Who are you most like in your family? (In what ways are you similar?)
- Do you go on holiday with your family? (Why? / Why not?)
- Have you done anything interesting with your friends recently? (What did you do with them?)
- Tell me about a really good friend of yours. (Do you share the same interests?)

Your interests
- Is there a sport or hobby you enjoy doing? (What do you do?) (Why do you like it?)
- If you could learn a new skill, what would you choose to do? (Why?)
- Do you like reading? (What do you read?) (Why do you like it?)
- Have you seen a good film recently? (Tell me about it.)

Future plans
- Have you got any plans for this weekend? (What are you going to do?)
- Are you going to go on holiday this year? (Where are you going to go?)
- Is there anything you'd like to study in the future? (Why?)
- Which country would you most like to visit in the future? (Do you think you'll go there one day?) (Why? / Why not?)

Part 2   4 minutes (6 minutes for groups of three)

Beautiful places
Listening to music

Interlocutor:	In this part of the test, I'm going to give each of you two photographs. I'd like you to talk about your photographs on your own for about a minute, and also to answer a question about your partner's photographs.
	(Candidate A), it's your turn first. Here are your photographs. They show people spending time in different beautiful places.
	Indicate the pictures on page C10 to the candidates.
	I'd like you to compare the photographs, and say what the people are enjoying about spending time in these beautiful places.
	All right?
Candidate A:	*[1 minute.]*
Interlocutor:	Thank you.
	(Candidate B), do you enjoy spending time in the countryside? ...... (Why? / Why not?)
Candidate B:	*[Approximately 30 seconds.]*
Interlocutor:	Thank you.
	Now, *(Candidate B)*, here are your photographs. They show people listening to music in different situations.
	Indicate the pictures on page C11 to the candidates.
	I'd like you to compare the photographs, and say why you think the people are listening to music in these situations.
	All right?
Candidate B:	*[1 minute.]*
Interlocutor:	Thank you.
	(Candidate A), would you like to go to a classical concert? ...... (Why? / Why not?)
Candidate A:	*[Approximately 30 seconds.]*
Interlocutor:	Thank you.

Parts 3 and 4   8 minutes (11 minutes for groups of three)

Part 3

Holiday at home

Interlocutor:	Now, I'd like you to talk about something together for about two minutes *(3 minutes for groups of three)*.
	Some people spend their holidays in their own country, instead of travelling to other countries. Here are some things they think about and a question for you to discuss. First you have some time to look at the task.
	Indicate the text on page C12 to the candidates. Allow 15 seconds.
	Now, talk to each other about whether people should have holidays in their own country instead of travelling to other countries.
Candidates:	*[2 minutes (3 minutes for groups of three).]*
Interlocutor:	Thank you. Now you have about a minute to decide what you think is the best reason for having a holiday in your country.
Candidates:	*[1 minute (for pairs and groups of three).]*
Interlocutor:	Thank you.

Part 4

Interlocutor: Use the following questions, in order, as appropriate:

- Where do people in your country go on their holidays? (Why do they like it there?)

- Some people say that holidays are for having fun, not for learning about other cultures. What do you think?

> *Select any of the following prompts, as appropriate:*
>
> - What do you think?
> - Do you agree?
> - And you?

- Do you think it's best to have one long holiday each year or several short ones? (Why?)

- Do you think it is important to find out a lot of information about the place you are visiting on holiday? (Why? / Why not?)

- Is it a good idea to go on holiday to the same place every year? (Why? / Why not?)

- Do you think it is important to speak the language of the country you are visiting? (Why? / Why not?)

Thank you. That is the end of the test.

Marks and results

Reading and Use of English

Candidates record their answers on a separate answer sheet. One mark is given for each correct answer in Parts 1, 2, 3 and 7. For Part 4, candidates are awarded a mark of 2, 1 or 0 for each question according to the accuracy of their response. Correct spelling is required in Parts 2, 3 and 4. Two marks are given for each correct answer in Parts 5 and 6.

Candidates will receive separate scores for Reading and for Use of English. The total marks candidates achieve for each section are converted into a score on the Cambridge English Scale. These are equally weighted when calculating the overall score on the scale (an average of the individual scores for the four skills and Use of English).

Writing

Examiners look at four aspects of your writing: Content, Communicative Achievement, Organisation and Language.

- Content focuses on how well you have fulfilled the task, in other words if you have done what you were asked to do.
- Communicative Achievement focuses on how appropriate the writing is for the task and whether you have used the appropriate register.
- Organisation focuses on the way you put the piece of writing together, in other words if it is logical and ordered.
- Language focuses on your vocabulary and grammar. This includes the range of language as well as how accurate it is.

For each of the subscales, the examiner gives a maximum of 5 marks. Examiners use the following assessment scale:

B2	Content	Communicative Achievement	Organisation	Language
5	All content is relevant to the task. Target reader is fully informed.	Uses the conventions of the communicative task effectively to hold the target reader's attention and communicate straightforward and complex ideas, as appropriate.	Text is well organised and coherent, using a variety of cohesive devices and organisational patterns to generally good effect.	Uses a range of vocabulary, including less common lexis, appropriately. Uses a range of simple and complex grammatical forms with control and flexibility. Occasional errors may be present but do not impede communication.
4	*Performance shares features of Bands 3 and 5.*			

3	Minor irrelevances and/or omissions may be present. Target reader is on the whole informed.	Uses the conventions of the communicative task to hold the target reader's attention and communicate straightforward ideas.	Text is generally well organised and coherent, using a variety of linking words and cohesive devices.	Uses a range of everyday vocabulary appropriately, with occasional inappropriate use of less common lexis. Uses a range of simple and some complex grammatical forms with a good degree of control. Errors do not impede communication.
2	*Performance shares features of Bands 1 and 3.*			
1	Irrelevances and misinterpretation of task may be present. Target reader is minimally informed.	Uses the conventions of the communicative task in generally appropriate ways to communicate straightforward ideas.	Text is connected and coherent, using basic linking words and a limited number of cohesive devices.	Uses everyday vocabulary generally appropriately, while occasionally overusing certain lexis. Uses simple grammatical forms with a good degree of control. While errors are noticeable, meaning can still be determined.
0	Content is totally irrelevant. Target reader is not informed.	*Performance below Band 1.*		

Length of responses

Make sure you write the correct number of words. Responses which are too short may not have an adequate range of language and may not provide all the information that is required. Responses which are too long may contain irrelevant content and have a negative effect on the reader.

Varieties of English

You are expected to use a particular variety of English with some degree of consistency in areas such as spelling, and not for example switch from using a British spelling of a word to an American spelling of the same word.

Writing sample answers and examiner's comments

The following pieces of writing have been selected from students' answers. The samples relate to tasks in Tests 1–4. Explanatory notes have been added to show how the bands have been arrived at.

Sample A (Test 1, Question 1 – Essay)

> *Famous sport people are getting a lot of money because their jobs is to entertain us the watcher. So it explained why they got a lot of money. It's their job to entertain us with their skills, and that is why they got paid well.*
>
> *I guess I don't agree that famous sport people got paid too much, well because what they can do sometimes can injured them like for instance boxer, yes that they do entertain us, but they can hurt each other such as make their opponent bleed, and it will cost them a fortune if something bad happens to them, and they can get broke if everytime they got an injury, and they got paid a little.*
>
> *I think that famous sport people really work hard, because like Kobe Bryant he shoots hundreds basketball to make sure he can a get a perfect by up, or Christiano Ronaldo he shoots hundred of balls to the gol to make sure he always strike when there's a penalty. Famous sport people really worked hard to entertain us, so no wonder they get paid a lot*
>
> *I guess it's fair ratio what they did, and their effort to keep us being entertain and what they earn because they deserve it. When they have a match, when their all sweaty and watch them score is an entertaining to do, and we can bet if the team that we are holding.*
>
> *When we're on a holiday they keep practicing, or they keep having match to entertain us, so they are really worked hard to earn that loads of money, so I guess that is why they deserve them.*

Scales	Mark	Commentary
Content	5	All content is relevant to the task. The target reader is fully informed about the two given points and the writer's own idea, the risk of injury.
Communicative Achievement	3	The writer uses the conventions of an essay to express personal opinions on the topic. Straightforward ideas are communicated and the writer's opinion is clear. The reader's attention is held, despite some confusion of the message arising from errors and poor control of organisation.
Organisation	3	The text is generally well organised and coherent using a variety of linking words and cohesive devices to generally good effect, although there is some loss of control in longer sentences, for example in the second paragraph.
Language	3	A range of vocabulary is used appropriately (*make their opponent bleed*; *cost them a fortune*; *an injury*; *sweaty*; *no wonder*; *loads of money*). There is a range of simple and some more complex grammatical forms. Although there are some errors, with choice and control of past tenses for example, these do not impede communication.

Sample B (Test 1, Question 2 – Report)

> *In a busy environment such as cities and towns, parks and green spaces plays an important role sheltering us from the pollution and giving a place to relax and feel connected with nature.*
>
> *Maputo is considered the town of "Acacias" a kind of tree that grows there, from the name it's easy to say that the city it's filled with trees and green spaces. Besides that, you can easily encounter beautiful parks with ancient trees, 100 years old.*
>
> *In order to improve those green spaces, it should start by doing sensitization campaigns telling to the citizens how important are those places to their well being. Another interesting way would be linking those parks with some economical activities in order to make it self sustainable.*
>
> *Being aware about the environment surrounding it's a start for a good citizenship. People's life will have improved significantly starting from having a good pure and fresh air to a place to relax. All in all, if the green stuff thrive, people thrive together.*

Scales	Mark	Commentary
Content	5	All content is relevant. The target reader is fully informed about the green areas and recommended improvements.
Communicative Achievement	4	The writer uses the conventions of report writing effectively. The tone is neutral and the argument is convincing, using an appropriate balance of information and personal comments and recommendations. The opening statement about the importance of green spaces is echoed in the concluding comments, which engages and holds the reader's attention.
Organisation	3	The text is generally well organised and coherent. Each point is addressed in a separate paragraph and a variety of linking words and cohesive devices are used (*such as; In order to improve those green spaces; Another interesting way would be; All in all*), with some less appropriate use (*the city it's filled; Besides that; those parks … make it self*).
Language	4	A range of vocabulary is used appropriately (*encounter; well being; sustainable; thrive*) with occasional inappropriate use due to ambition (*sensitization; economical activities; environment surrounding*). There is a range of simple and complex grammatical forms, including passive and modal structures and a range of tenses, used with control. Errors do not impede communication.

Sample C (Test 2, Question 1 – Essay)

> *Choosing whether to be self-employed or to work for somebody else can be a difficult decision, but there are advantages and disadvantages in both cases.*
>
> *Working for someone else is the most common method of earning money. You depend on our employer, but you are offered security to a certain degree. You are never safe from being fired but you have a source of income as long as you are not unemployed.*
>
> *Being self-employed can go two ways: you are either successful or your business goes bankrupt. Some businesses that were started by a handful of people can turn into corporations worth millions, maybe billions of dollars. If you work for yourself, you are independent and the only person you depend on is yourself. You can also be on the verge of bankruptcy, but if you know how to manage your own business, you can be successful.*
>
> *To conclude, there is no definitive answer. Go with what choice seems natural to you and you can be successful either way!*

Scales	Mark	Commentary
Content	5	All content is relevant to the task. The reader is fully informed about the two given points and the writer's own idea, managing financial matters.
Communicative Achievement	5	The essay is well-controlled and persuasive, following the conventions of essay writing effectively. There is a clear introduction, a balanced argument of both straightforward and complex ideas and a strong concluding comment. The tone is neutral and consistent and engages and holds the target reader's attention effectively.
Organisation	4	The text is well organised and coherent. Topic sentences effectively introduce each new point and the structure of the argument is clearly signalled using cohesive devices and organisational patterns, such as parallel structures (*in both cases; can go two ways; either … or; To conclude; either way*). A greater variety of cohesive devices and more effective use of paragraphing would benefit the overall cohesion of the text.
Language	5	There is a range of everyday and less common lexis used appropriately and with flexibility (*to a certain degree; goes bankrupt; on the verge of bankruptcy; definitive answer*). A range of simple and more complex grammatical forms, such as passive structures, gerunds and conditionals, is used with control and flexibility and errors are minimal.

Sample D (Test 2, Question 4 – Email)

> Hi,
>
> I'm glad you asked for my help! My cousin had the same problem. Home or university? That is the question. The answer depends on many things but mostly your plans for the future. Let me tell you what happened to Jake (this is the cousin's name). He had one hobby, maths. He always knew that his job will be conected with it. In the age of 15 Jake didn't want to learn anything else! One day he had an exam but so important one that it was organised only in the capital of Poland. Unfortunetely, Jake was late. Before he went to sleep, he has had forgotten to ask his mother to wake him up. The train had left before he got to the station. Then he called his teacher and asked them for a second chance. They agreed! When he wrote the test, everybody was so impressed about his skills that he got an offert-"be the student of our university. We want you". Then he had to choose. Staying with family or going abroad? He prefered home and trust me, it was a huge mistake. And that's what you should do-follow your dreams.
>
> See you soon
>
> Inga

Scales	Mark	Commentary
Content	5	All content is relevant to the task. Although the story about the writer's cousin does not directly address the target reader's question, it is relevant and final comment ensures the reader is fully informed.
Communicative Achievement	4	The text follows the conventions of the communicative task with a chatty style and effective use of informal language. By directly addressing the reader and using rhetorical questions, the writer engages and holds the reader's attention throughout.
Organisation	3	The text is generally well organised and coherent. There is a range of cohesive devices, including referencing pronouns, used generally appropriately, but paragraphing would be helpful in separating the anecdote from the response to the reader's question.
Language	3	There is a range of everyday vocabulary used appropriately, despite some spelling errors. There is a range of simple and some more complex grammatical forms, including past perfect structures, used with a good degree of control. Errors do not impede communication.

Sample E (Test 3, Question 1 – Essay)

We live in 21st century and advertising is part of our lives. We watch TV we read newspapers, even when we drive we can see advertisments.

Usually advertisments are very helpul. For example food advertising. People need to know what product they are buying and if it is good not only for their health but also for their budget. When they SEE the advertisment, they will know if they product is worth buying. Personally I think advertisment are a very good way for keeping PEOPLE informed.

But I think there is a bad side too. Compaies organize some kind of competitions between themselves and maybe this is good for the companies but not for the people. They get bored when two or more companies start a competition and they also get confused, because one company can give you something, the other can not but the second one can give you something, the first can not. So after all this competing, people do not know which company to choose.

Another bad side of advertising is that advertisments show us only the good side of the product. But WE can not be sure this is good for us. Also advertisments can be really annoying for people because like I said they are everywhere. It is not really good when you are watching your favourite show and they stop it for a minute or two just to advertise some new products or companies.

To sum up I think sometimes advertising is helpful but it is not nessassary to be such important part of our lives.

Scales	Mark	Commentary
Content	5	All content is relevant and the target reader is fully informed about the two given points and the writer's own ideas, how advertising may not always be true and may also be intrusive.
Communicative Achievement	5	The writer has presented a well-balanced argument, with examples and explanations to support ideas, fulfilling the communicative purpose of essay writing and holding the target reader's attention. Straightforward and complex ideas, for example when discussing competition between companies in the third paragraph, are communicated effectively.
Organisation	5	The text is well organised and coherent. The structure of the essay is clearly signalled and ideas are connected effectively at sentence and paragraph level by a variety of cohesive devices and organisational patterns, including referencing and ellipsis (*not only … but also; this is good for … but not for; one company can … the other can not; So after all this competing; like I said*).
Language	5	There is a range of vocabulary, including some less common lexis, used appropriately (*budget; worth buying; get bored*), despite some slips with spelling. A range of simple and more complex grammatical forms, such as passives and verb patterns, is used with control. Occasional errors do not impede communication.

Sample F (Test 3, Question 2 – Article)

> To start I will mention that I am not a person who likes changes, I prefer to plan everything, my everyday tasks, homework, and hours; even though I have divided my day using my cell phone which remainds me what to do every minute of my busy schedule. But to be honest many sudden and unplanned changes have modified my life.
>
> Twenty years ago I got pregnant and I had a beautiful baby, he changed my perspective of everything. Due to this event I started to work as an english teacher because during that time I was only studying. I got involved in a job environment, running from one place to another and it was beginning of my obsetion with the arrangement of time. As a result of my incursion in teaching I began to "live into English". I took as many english courses as I could, and without noticing I began to love more and more the language.
>
> Four years ago I decided to start a major in Foreing Languages and improve my english level. Nowadays I have learnt a lot of techniques to use while I am teaching, I have learnt a bit about British English but in addition to this I have learnt French, a new completly language for me.
>
> In sum I do not like changes but having a son and starting a new major have been the most exciting events that have been transforming my life, and thanks to them I have fought for and achieved the things that I have now

Scales	Mark	Commentary
Content	5	All content is relevant to the task. The target reader is fully informed about the writer's attitude to and personal experience of change.
Communicative Achievement	3	The writer uses the conventions of an article to hold the reader's attention and communicate straightforward opinions and experiences. The points are developed appropriately with examples and explanations and there is a clear conclusion. Also including a general introduction to the topic would be appropriate.
Organisation	3	The text is generally well organised with suitable paragraphing and a variety of linking words and cohesive devices used, generally appropriately, to introduce and connect ideas (*To start; But to be honest; because during that time; from one place to another; As a result of; in addition to this; thanks to them*).
Language	3	A range of everyday and some less common vocabulary is used appropriately (*unplanned changes; modified my life; perspective; transforming my life*), although there are some spelling errors and occasional inappropriate use of less common lexis (*incursion in teaching; live into English*). There is a range of simple and some more complex grammatical forms used with a good degree of control. Errors, for example with articles and word order, do not impede communication.

Sample G (Test 4, Question 1 – Essay)

> It is good or bad thing to have products that last a long time; sometimes make us on a doubt about Products with long life like batteries, tvs, computers, clothes, acessories,ect.
>
> Fashion for example is always changing and it is difficult to follow it. Changing technology is a good idea because the usefull of the device has a time of use. And when it is over the device doesnot work properly. About bowls, mugs and so on, sometimes is good to keep them, especially if you had taken it for a special moment.
>
> I think you need to have a common sense to Keep things, other wise we become an accumulator person and it is really bad for us and for the community we live.
>
> Furthermore, if you want to Keep many products for long time we need a space to Keep them.
>
> In conclusion, if have long-lasting products is good or bad depends on the people who has it. In adiction people need to be conscious about the planet, because most of long-lasting products are dangerous for the soil and the air. We need to Know where leave these products, when they donot work anymore.

Scales	Mark	Commentary
Content	5	All content is relevant and the target reader would be fully informed. The two given points in the question are addressed and the writer has included more than one 'own idea': sentimental reasons; storage and environmental issues.
Communicative Achievement	3	The conventions of essay writing, including a consistent neutral tone and suitable introduction and conclusion, are used appropriately. The writer combines general comments with a personal response to the topic, holding the target reader's attention and communicating straightforward ideas.
Organisation	3	The text is generally well organised and coherent with suitable paragraphing and generally appropriate use of a variety of linking words (*because; other wise; Furthermore; In conclusion; in addiction*) and cohesive devices, including referencing pronouns. A greater variety of cohesive devices to connect ideas in longer sentences, for example in the second paragraph, would improve the overall cohesiveness of the text.
Language	2	There is a range of everyday vocabulary used appropriately (*device; a special moment; common sense; long-lasting; conscious; soil*), with occasional inappropriate use of less common vocabulary. A range of simple grammatical forms is used with reasonable control. Errors with lexis and structure are distracting at times, but the meaning can still be determined (*sometimes make us on a doubt about; the usefull of the device has a time of use; if have long-lasting product is good or bad depends on the people who has it*).

Sample H (Test 4, Question 3 – Review)

> I had recently been to on art museum in Cluj-Napoca and it was an amazing experience!
>
> The art exhibition had the abstract theme and it succeeded in giving me the emotions which the paintings suggest. For example, there was a painting called "The Guide to Loneliness" which had a man standing in the corner of an obscure room containing only a bed and undistinguishable details on the walls. This painting really made me feel sad and lonely, so I guess the reason which I found the exhibition interesting for war its' ability to give me the emotions that were represented in the paintings.
>
> I would recommend it to people who are into art and who are impressed not only by the way a painting looks, but by the way it makes them feel like too. Although, I recommend this exhibition to patient people, as understanding a painting may take a while of thinking.

Scales	Mark	Commentary
Content	5	All content is relevant to the task and the target reader would be fully informed about the exhibition, the writer's impression and who it would be suitable for.
Communicative Achievement	4	The text follows the conventions of review writing to engage the reader and communicate straightforward and some more complex ideas, for example when describing the writer's reactions to one of the paintings. The communicative purposes of describing, explaining and recommending are fulfilled.
Organisation	3	The text is generally well organised and coherent. Paragraphing is used effectively to structure the key points in the review and there is a range of cohesive devices, including referencing and ellipsis, used generally appropriately.
Language	4	Everyday and less common, topic-specific, vocabulary is used generally appropriately (*abstract theme; Loneliness; obscure room; undistinguishable; impressed*). There is a range of simple and complex grammatical forms, including a variety of tenses, modals, passive structures and relative clauses. Where there are errors, these do not impede communication.

Listening

One mark is given for each correct answer. The total mark is converted into a score on the Cambridge English Scale for the paper. In Part 2, minor spelling errors are allowed, provided that the candidate's intention is clear.

For security reasons, several versions of the Listening paper are used at each administration of the examination. Before grading, the performance of the candidates in each of the versions is compared and marks adjusted to compensate for any imbalance in levels of difficulty.

Speaking

Throughout the test candidates are assessed on their own individual performance and not in relation to the other candidate. They are assessed on their language skills, not on their personality, intelligence or knowledge of the world. Candidates must, however, be prepared to develop the conversation and respond to the tasks in an appropriate way.

Candidates are awarded marks by two examiners: the assessor and the interlocutor. The assessor awards marks by applying performance descriptors from the Analytical Assessment scales for the following criteria:

Grammar and Vocabulary
This refers to the accurate use of grammatical forms and appropriate use of vocabulary. It also includes the range of language.

Discourse Management
This refers to the extent, relevance and coherence of each candidate's contributions. Candidates should be able to construct clear stretches of speech which are easy to follow. The length of their contributions should be appropriate to the task, and what they say should be related to the topic and the conversation in general.

Pronunciation
This refers to the intelligibility of contributions at word and sentence levels. Candidates should be able to produce utterances that can easily be understood, and which show control of intonation, stress and individual sounds.

Interactive Communication
This refers to the ability to use language to achieve meaningful communication. Candidates should be able to initiate and respond appropriately according to the task and conversation, and also to use interactive strategies to maintain and develop the communication whilst negotiating towards an outcome.

B2	Grammar and Vocabulary	Discourse Management	Pronunciation	Interactive Communication
5	• Shows a good degree of control of a range of simple and some complex grammatical forms. • Uses a range of appropriate vocabulary to give and exchange views on a wide range of familiar topics.	• Produces extended stretches of language with very little hesitation. • Contributions are relevant and there is a clear organisation of ideas. • Uses a range of cohesive devices and discourse markers.	• Is intelligible. • Intonation is appropriate. • Sentence and word stress is accurately placed. • Individual sounds are articulated clearly.	• Initiates and responds appropriately, linking contributions to those of other speakers. • Maintains and develops the interaction and negotiates towards an outcome.
4	*Performance shares features of Bands 3 and 5.*			
3	• Shows a good degree of control of simple grammatical forms, and attempts some complex grammatical forms. • Uses a range of appropriate vocabulary to give and exchange views on a range of familiar topics.	• Produces extended stretches of language despite some hesitation. • Contributions are relevant and there is very little repetition. • Uses a range of cohesive devices.	• Is intelligible. • Intonation is generally appropriate. • Sentence and word stress is generally accurately placed. • Individual sounds are generally articulated clearly.	• Initiates and responds appropriately. • Maintains and develops the interaction and negotiates towards an outcome with very little support.
2	*Performance shares features of Bands 1 and 3.*			
1	• Shows a good degree of control of simple grammatical forms. • Uses a range of appropriate vocabulary when talking about everyday situations.	• Produces responses which are extended beyond short phrases, despite hesitation. • Contributions are mostly relevant, despite some repetition. • Uses basic cohesive devices.	• Is mostly intelligible, and has some control of phonological features at both utterance and word levels.	• Initiates and responds appropriately. • Keeps the interaction going with very little prompting and support.
0	*Performance below Band 1.*			

The interlocutor awards a mark for overall performance using a Global Achievement scale.

B2	Global Achievement
5	• Handles communication on a range of familiar topics, with very little hesitation. • Uses accurate and appropriate linguistic resources to express ideas and produce extended discourse that is generally coherent.
4	*Performance shares features of Bands 3 and 5.*
3	• Handles communication on familiar topics, despite some hesitation. • Organises extended discourse but occasionally produces utterances that lack coherence, and some inaccuracies and inappropriate usage occur.
2	*Performance shares features of Bands 1 and 3.*
1	• Handles communication in everyday situations, despite hesitation. • Constructs longer utterances but is not able to use complex language except in well-rehearsed utterances.
0	*Performance below Band 1.*

Assessment for *Cambridge English: First* is based on performance across all parts of the test, and is achieved by applying the relevant descriptors in the assessment scales.

Test 1 Key

Reading and Use of English (1 hour 15 minutes)

Part 1

1 D   2 D   3 A   4 C   5 B   6 B   7 A   8 D

Part 2

9 of   10 one   11 whether/if   12 Because   13 have   14 from
15 in   16 rather

Part 3

17 variety   18 emotional   19 satisfaction   20 impossible
21 importance   22 creativity   23 preparation   24 pleasure

Part 4

25 HAS a shower | before going
26 if she | had not / hadn't BEEN OR had she | not BEEN
27 not go / be / be put / be going | on SALE
28 eats / will eat / likes all VEGETABLES | apart
29 have/get the/his spelling | CHECKED by
30 EXCUSE me (for)/my | disturbing

Part 5

31 A   32 D   33 B   34 D   35 A   36 A

Part 6

37 F   38 C   39 E   40 G   41 B   42 D

Part 7

43 C   44 A   45 D   46 B   47 D   48 D   49 C   50 B   51 B   52 A

Writing (1 hour 20 minutes)

Candidate responses are marked using the assessment scale on pages 107–108.

Listening (approximately 40 minutes)

Part 1

1 A   2 A   3 B   4 B   5 B   6 C   7 B   8 C

Part 2

9 father   10 humour/humor   11 plants   12 (physical) size
13 panic   14 (plastic) bags   15 knife   16 river
17 fire (without matches)   18 (being good at) time management

Part 3

19 G   20 F   21 A   22 H   23 C

Part 4

24 C   25 A   26 C   27 C   28 C   29 B   30 A

Transcript   *This is the Cambridge English: First Listening Test. Test One.*

I'm going to give you the instructions for this test. I'll introduce each part of the test and give you time to look at the questions. At the start of each piece you will hear this sound:

tone

You'll hear each piece twice.

Remember, while you're listening, write your answers on the question paper. You'll have five minutes at the end of the test to copy your answers onto the separate answer sheet.

There will now be a pause. Please ask any questions now, because you must not speak during the test.

[pause]

Now open your question paper and look at Part One.

[pause]

PART 1   *You'll hear people talking in eight different situations. For questions 1 to 8, choose the best answer (A, B or C).*

Question 1   *You hear a woman talking on the radio about an actor.*

[pause]

tone

Woman: Like many actors, he always seems to be in the news for one reason or another. I know celebrities can be given a tough time, but he seems to get off relatively lightly. He's in loads of movies these days – and so he should be. His performances were fairly patchy when he was starting out, in my opinion, but that's never the case these days. And the signs are he'll continue to develop, especially now he's getting to play lead roles in popular theatre productions, too. If you ever get the chance to see him on stage, you won't be disappointed. Otherwise, catch him at a cinema near you!

[pause]

tone

[The recording is repeated.]

[pause]

Question 2   *You hear a hairstylist talking about her career.*

[pause]

tone

Man: You initially started off doing the hair of models in the fashion industry. What made you move to TV?

Woman: The fashion industry turned me off quite a bit actually. I didn't like working with people who had such a high opinion of themselves. My attitude is that you should treat everyone the same and I found I was constantly having to bite my tongue because of the way I was treated there. The TV's different: it's much more a case of being respected for what you can offer regardless of your status ... and that suits me. The TV people acknowledge you as a fellow professional and they're much more down-to-earth.

[pause]

tone

[The recording is repeated.]

[pause]

Question 3   *You hear a comedian called Geoff Knight talking on the radio about his profession.*

[pause]

tone

Man: When I'm doing my comedy act, at theatres or clubs or on TV, I'll often get my ideas from keeping my ears close to the ground. I try to pick up on all the strange and humorous everyday stuff, sometimes even boring … that you get in life … and I build it into my act. Obviously I do also get ideas from listening to other comedians too. I like to think that three generations of one family can sit at my show and know they won't feel threatened, because I'm not rude. Even in big arenas people feel like I'm talking to them individually. It's a comfort thing for them.

[pause]

tone

[The recording is repeated.]

[pause]

Question 4   *You hear a conversation between a customer and a coffee shop employee.*

[pause]

tone

Woman: Excuse me. Could someone come over and clear one of the tables in the window please?

Man: Oh yes. I'm sorry. We've just had a really busy lunch break and, between you and me, my colleague's new and hasn't really got the hang of things yet.

Woman: Yes, you look as if you've been really busy.

Man: We should be able to get straight now it's a bit quieter. I'll get my colleague to come and clear your table right away.

Woman: Hmmm … It certainly needs it!

Man: Anyway, what can I get you? Coffee and cake or …

Woman: I'll just have coffee please.

Man: And I'll get a cloth to wipe the table.

[pause]

tone

[The recording is repeated.]

[pause]

Question 5   *You hear a man telling a friend about an art exhibition.*

[pause]

tone

Woman: Hi Mark, how did you like the exhibition?

Man: It was alright, actually. I've got the catalogue here. Would you like to have a look?

Woman: I don't usually bother with them, personally. They've always felt like a bit of a waste of money.

Man: I know what you mean, but somebody lent me this one.

Woman: So ... what's the gallery like?

Man: Really cool, using natural light to show off the paintings – saves energy too, you know ...

Woman: I expect it was crowded.

Man: Well, I'd expected there to be masses of people, so I wouldn't be able to see anything. In fact, I nearly had the place to myself.

[pause]

tone

[The recording is repeated.]

[pause]

Question 6   *You overhear a man ringing a sports shop.*

[pause]

tone

Man: Hello. Colin Foggerty here. I was in the shop last week, and bought a pair of the new Comfort football boots. I asked about a discount I'd heard about for members of Kirkley Rangers football club, which I'm a member of. The assistant was by herself and said she didn't know anything about it. I then checked on the football club website, and it confirms what I thought. I emailed you at the shop this morning and was told that the shop gives special discounts for official club purchases, but I'm still not sure whether the discount is applicable to ordinary club members like me. So I thought I'd better ring and sort it all out.

[pause]

tone

[The recording is repeated.]

[pause]

Question 7   *You hear a man telling a friend about his work.*

[pause]

tone

Woman: So you've been at the company for five years, how do you feel it's going?

Man: Well, the boss sees me as someone who'll go far but I don't really know if I want to. I mean I've seen what happened to Joe who was promoted last year to sales manager. At the time, I thought 'lucky him', but he isn't enjoying it. The working environment isn't as friendly and supportive as it was when I first joined – mainly because of all the targets we've been set. Sad that management feels the need to play with what was a winning formula. Still, let's see what the future brings.

[pause]

tone

[The recording is repeated.]

[pause]

Question 8   *You hear two people talking about a country walk they're doing.*

[pause]

tone

Man: Are you feeling tired?

Woman: No, I'm fine, just stopping to look at the scenery. It's beautiful, isn't it?

Man: Fabulous, but keep moving – it's too cold to stand still.

Woman: Well, we knew that when we set off. The forecast's better for tomorrow. I did say we should wait.

Man: Sorry, I know, but let's carry on because there's only another five kilometres to go. Right or left here?

Woman: Left, I think, according to the map. Five kilometres you said? It'll be just about dark when we get to the end.

Man: If we do get there! I'm only joking!

[pause]

tone

[The recording is repeated.]

[pause]

That's the end of Part One.

Now turn to Part Two.

[pause]

PART 2   *You'll hear a presentation given by a university student called Megan Rowlings about a forest survival course she went on in Australia. For questions 9 to 18, complete the sentences with a word or short phrase.*

You now have forty-five seconds to look at Part Two.

[pause]

tone

Hi, my name's Megan and I'm going to tell you about a forest survival course in Australia. So how did I come to do a course like that? Well, I'd been thinking about what to do in my summer holiday and my professor suggested I should do some teaching at a summer camp he was running, but I wanted to get away from academic stuff for a while. Then my father found the website about survival courses while looking for something to interest my brother. And that was it!

The course leader, John, was a very experienced survival expert with an impressive range of skills. I can't tell you how absolutely terrifying the experience of being in the forest was at times but John's humour eased the tension, for which I was really grateful. He also knew exactly when to offer support and when to leave us to it.

Chris was his assistant, and he brought different qualities to the group. He was never short of enthusiasm, and was particularly keen on insects – he told us the name of every one we came across in the forest. He also knew all the facts about plants so that over the five days, we got to know what was safe to eat while we were there and what we had to avoid. That information proved really valuable.

There were ten of us on the course and we made a great team. I thought I'd struggle with the tasks that made big physical demands because of my size, but I soon learnt that mental toughness was equally important. And in fact that turned out to be something I didn't have a problem with.

John drilled into us the importance of staying safe at all times. In that respect, possessing sufficient self-awareness is key … knowing our own capabilities and limitations could save our lives. All this holds back panic, which is often a greater danger than the situations we find ourselves in.

We'd all been equipped with a mini survival kit which contained things like a first aid kit and water sterilisation tablets, and of course we'd all brought other things as well, including some fancy gadgets which were never used … but nobody else had thought about plastic bags to keep stuff dry in our rucksacks. I passed mine around and they were much appreciated.

Our first task was to make tools that we could use. For example, did you know you can actually make a spear from a branch if it's strong enough? We were shown how to make a knife out of a stone that was lying on the forest floor. It took me quite a long time to make one but it was great for all sorts of tasks.

The next thing was to find a water source. We found a small stream and we followed that some distance to where it finally joined a river. John told us that because the water at that point was quite fast-flowing, it was drinkable as long as we boiled it. There was also a small lake nearby but we were advised not to use that because of the wild animals that were often there.

Our first meal in the forest was what we collected ourselves, such as berries. Then, after all that walking and looking for food, we were ready for a good night's sleep. I didn't find making a shelter too problematic actually, which was just as well because if lighting a fire without matches had been left to me, then we'd have been shivering all night!

The thing that I found most interesting about the course was that many of the skills I use as a student at university are invaluable for survival too. Of course, you'd expect team-building to be useful. But what I hadn't expected was that being good at time management would also be an advantage.

[pause]

Now you'll hear Part Two again.

tone

[The recording is repeated.]

[pause]

That's the end of Part Two.

Now turn to Part Three.

[pause]

PART 3   *You'll hear five short extracts in which people talk about a problem they had in their first few weeks in a new job. For questions 19 to 23, choose what problem (A to H) each speaker says they had. Use the letters only once. There are three extra letters which you do not need to use.*

You now have thirty seconds to look at Part Three.

[pause]

tone

Speaker 1

Well I work for an IT company and I love it because it's really stimulating. I work hard but the rewards are there. At the same time it's quite laid back – at least where the dress code is concerned anyway. My first few weeks were great. My friend works in the adjoining building so we often had lunch together. The problem was, she had a longer lunch break than me and I started wandering back a few minutes over the hour. I didn't think anyone would notice but my colleagues soon had a quiet word with me – in the nicest possible way of course! I don't do that anymore.

[pause]

Speaker 2

My first job was for a finance company. I'd beaten off quite a few candidates to get the job and I was riding high. I'd bought a new suit and briefcase and walked in there on the first day thinking 'This is it. Now I'm going to show them what I'm made of.' I thought I knew it all. I'd correct colleagues if they said something wrong and I was always talking about what I'd learnt at university. Anyway, in my fourth week the boss called me in and told me I'd done something that had lost the company quite a lot of money. I learnt a lot that day.

[pause]

Speaker 3

I worked for a small company locally. It was my first job back after maternity leave and I was really glad to be back at work. I got on well with my colleagues and the work was fine, but I really didn't like the boss. Anyway, I got quite friendly in the first few weeks with the receptionist. She was a nice young girl – very chatty. She asked me how I was getting on and I said I really liked the job and everything, but not the boss. Stupid I know. Anyway, it turns out that the receptionist was the boss's niece! Small world. I should've noticed their surnames were the same!

[pause]

Speaker 4

Well, I didn't really need the job in the supermarket. You know, I was retired and just wanted something to fill the time and the extra money was useful. I'd been a manager for an engineering company in the past so I knew how things worked. I did my job. I was always on time. But I resented being told to do things that weren't in my job description, and I didn't think that was fair. I didn't say anything but I think they knew I wasn't happy. In the end, I decided I didn't fit in. On reflection, I think retirement suits me better.

[pause]

Speaker 5

I've never been very confident so I was really surprised when I was offered a job in a very posh law company. I decided to really show them that I was up to doing the job, but I went a bit too far – volunteering to do everything, taking clients' names and details home to memorise so I could greet them by name when they came in and so on. I overdid it actually because I wasn't being myself. After a few weeks, my colleagues told me to relax and that I was doing fine as I was. I didn't need to prove anything. I love my job now.

[pause]

Now you'll hear Part Three again.

tone

[The recording is repeated.]

[pause]

That's the end of Part Three.

Now turn to Part Four.

[pause]

PART 4   *You'll hear an interview with an international concert pianist called Karen Hong. For questions 24 to 30, choose the best answer (A, B or C).*

You now have one minute to look at Part Four.

[pause]

tone

Interviewer:	My guest today is the international concert pianist, Karen Hong. Welcome Karen. I'm sure you're busy with your piano practice!
Karen:	Don't apologise! But you're right – I do an average of six hours' practice a day. People think when you're a performer, you just know the pieces of music by heart and don't need to practise, but this isn't true! For one thing, you might be performing a piece for the first time. For another, even pieces you know well still need maintenance and repair work on them. Also, every pianist at whatever level needs to do their drills and finger exercises as a warm-up.
Interviewer:	I remember you saying before that your parents are both very dynamic, motivated people.
Karen:	Yes absolutely. My mother would repeat to me 'You have this opportunity to develop your talent. Neither your father nor I had this. Don't waste it.' She made me do three hours' practice a day even before I was allowed out with my friends. She's never cared about the fame or fortune aspect of my career. To this day, she'll still tell me if she thinks I haven't done enough practice before a concert. Dad's different – he can't hide his delight at my success.
Interviewer:	You won a major competition for young musicians, and for a couple of years you seemed to be forever in the limelight.
Karen:	I got numerous offers to do advertising … even modelling! When you're thrown into all that, it's really easy to become disorientated and forget what brought you to everyone's attention in the first place. I reached a point where I didn't believe all the hype about me. I kept asking myself what my celebrity was really based on. I was doing more than 100 concerts a year so I didn't have nearly enough time to rehearse properly. I'd walk onto a stage and feel I was insulting my own ability.
Interviewer:	So you decided to take some time off, I believe?
Karen:	Yes, I felt some of the support I needed wasn't necessarily there within the profession. It's an extremely cut-throat business, so I guess it's understandable. So yes, I turned my back on that world for two months – gave no performances. I changed my agent, I found two new teachers in China, and I made sure I got back to practising with other pianists as opposed to by myself.
Interviewer:	At the time when you were performing a lot on TV, the media seemed to be using you to glamorise classical music.

Karen: Yes the marketing people tried to project me as a popular classical babe … you know trying to make classical music more youthful and appealing. And while I rejected all the glamour side of that, the purely musical aspect of it did still appeal to me. I love the idea of building a bridge between two worlds. I've played Bach at a televised rock concert in Russia! As long as I can play a piece of music that I think is good, I'm up for playing it anywhere.

Interviewer: So what do you feel about pop music?

Karen: I don't really have strong opinions about it – I just think it's a pity that in some countries there's this commercial culture attached to it that is drummed into kids' brains every day, and that this makes them see classical music as elitist and remote when subsequently they get to be teenagers. But to a five-year-old child, say, music is music. It just sounds how it should. They don't have any preconceptions about it.

Interviewer: I understand you've done a lot of work with young school children.

Karen: Yes, classical music can really help children to become happy, creative people. But when I go into schools I don't just say nice encouraging things to the children … the musicians ... when they don't deserve it. I went into one school regularly to help out with music lessons. And after a while I really started to emphasise to them the value of hard work. As a result the school now has nine of its students playing with the National Youth Orchestra.

[pause]

Now you'll hear Part Four again.

tone

[The recording is repeated.]

[pause]

That's the end of Part Four.

There will now be a pause of five minutes for you to copy your answers onto the separate answer sheet. Be sure to follow the numbering of all the questions. I'll remind you when there is one minute left so that you're sure to finish in time.

[Teacher, pause the recording here for five minutes. Remind students when they have one minute left.]

That's the end of the test. Please stop now. Your supervisor will now collect all the question papers and answer sheets.

Test 2 Key

Reading and Use of English (1 hour 15 minutes)

Part 1

1 C   2 D   3 B   4 C   5 A   6 C   7 B   8 D

Part 2

9 well   10 than   11 everyone/everybody   12 out   13 where   14 as
15 another   16 no

Part 3

17 popularity   18 scientific   19 requirements   20 exceptional   21 unfit
22 ability   23 obsession   24 acceptance

Part 4

25 was | the FIRST time
26 like/love to | be ABLE to
27 more crowded THAN | it used
28 how DEEP | the water / it is/gets
29 on (singing) | EVEN though/when
30 ever seen | SUCH a large

Part 5

31 A   32 A   33 C   34 B   35 A   36 C

Part 6

37 E   38 D   39 A   40 F   41 G   42 C

Part 7

43 C   44 E   45 D   46 B   47 A   48 B   49 E   50 D   51 A   52 C

Writing (1 hour 20 minutes)

Candidate responses are marked using the assessment scale on pages 107–108.

Listening (approximately 40 minutes)

Part 1

1 B   2 A   3 A   4 C   5 A   6 B   7 C   8 C

Part 2

9 uncle   10 main(-)land   11 marine science   12 swim
13 (the) transport   14 night   15 gentle   16 heat
17 concentration   18 returners

Part 3

19 C   20 H   21 F   22 B   23 E

Part 4

24 A   25 C   26 B   27 A   28 B   29 A   30 B

Transcript   *This is the Cambridge English: First Listening Test. Test Two.*

I'm going to give you the instructions for this test. I'll introduce each part of the test and give you time to look at the questions. At the start of each piece you will hear this sound:

tone

You'll hear each piece twice.

Remember, while you're listening, write your answers on the question paper. You'll have five minutes at the end of the test to copy your answers onto the separate answer sheet.

There will now be a pause. Please ask any questions now, because you must not speak during the test.

[pause]

Now open your question paper and look at Part One.

[pause]

PART 1   *You'll hear people talking in eight different situations. For questions 1 to 8, choose the best answer (A, B or C).*

Question 1   *You hear a man talking about collecting old coins.*

[pause]

tone

Man: My Dad used to collect rare old coins, and when I was younger I thought that was a really weird thing to do, but as I've got older I can see the attraction. Someone once bought a loaf of bread or some cheese with those coins, and for me that's brilliant. I don't buy online much because you never know what you're getting and there are a lot of fakes out there. I go to a specialist coin shop and chat to the guys there – they know everything there is to know about coins. I've got a few gaps in my collection but that's fine. I'm not one for perfection!

[pause]

tone

[The recording is repeated.]

[pause]

Question 2   *You hear a woman talking about playing the piano.*

[pause]

tone

Woman: People ask me about playing the piano and if it's a difficult instrument to learn, and the answer is yes and no. At the beginning, anyone can make a sound on the piano just by pressing a single note and it sounds pretty good – the equivalent could not be said about learning the violin, however. But to progress further, you have to have patience and some musical ability. It's best to learn from someone who knows, and is good at teaching, the technique needed. And obviously there's no escaping from the fact that you have to practise every day without fail. That way you'll come on quite quickly.

[pause]

tone

[The recording is repeated.]

[pause]

Question 3   You overhear a man and a woman talking in an art gallery about a boy's paintings.

[pause]

tone

Woman: It's hard to believe the artist's only seven years old! Look at the perspective in this one – he's got it just right. It takes art students years to master that.

Man: A child couldn't have painted these! I reckon it's all a fake. The gallery's passing off the paintings of someone much older as the work of a child – to trick people into buying. I mean, the way he's got the effect of the light on the water – that's the work of a much more experienced artist.

Woman: I saw a TV programme about him – he really does do them himself. And people must think they're worth the price – they're sold out.

[pause]

tone

[The recording is repeated.]

[pause]

Question 4   You hear two students talking about a university chemistry lecturer.

[pause]

tone

Woman: Hi Mike! That was another good chemistry lecture by Jane Wilson, wasn't it?

Man: Yeah, I like her. I can't always follow what she's saying, though.

Woman: Oh, I think she makes complicated ideas easier to understand. And she's so good at communicating her own excitement about chemistry – we all end up sharing it.

Man: There's no denying that. And she's okay about things like getting work in a few days after a deadline, which is nice.

Woman: That hasn't been everyone's experience, I must say. But then I can see why, really. Her schedule's so packed, I'm amazed she has time to do all she does.

Man: Yeah, that's true ...

[pause]

tone

[The recording is repeated.]

[pause]

Question 5	*You hear a woman talking to a work colleague about moving abroad for a new job.*
	[pause]
	tone
Man:	Two years living away is a long time!
Woman:	Yes, but I don't have to worry about whether I can return to my old position. That's guaranteed. Anyway, I'm 24 now and opportunities like this aren't common.
Man:	… Especially to oversee new project developments!
Woman:	Yes … I mean, I was doing that already, in a way, so I'm not sure I can think of it as a promotion. The only thing is, I tried to negotiate a delay to the contract so I'd have a bit more time to get myself together, but it couldn't be done. I felt I didn't have any say in the matter.
Man:	Oh well, don't let that get in the way!
	[pause]
	tone
	[The recording is repeated.]
	[pause]
Question 6	*You hear two friends talking about a job interview.*
	[pause]
	tone
Man:	Hi Noelle, how did the job interview go?
Woman:	Quite well, actually. Though I knew it would be alright.
Man:	Really?
Woman:	Well, yeah – I mean I'm usually nervous about job interviews, and there were three of them asking me questions! But this time, I felt very well prepared. And I've got the right kind of experience for the job, so that gave me confidence, I suppose.
Man:	Were there any questions you couldn't answer?
Woman:	Not really, though some were pretty hard! Luckily I'd done plenty of research beforehand. Clearly they hadn't expected me to be able to answer them all, so that was good.
Man:	Well I hope you get it!
Woman:	Thanks.
	[pause]
	tone
	[The recording is repeated.]
	[pause]

Question 7   *You hear part of a radio programme.*

[pause]

tone

Woman: I think lots of people will be interested in finding out more about it. It's a great way of seeing all the plants and trees that thrive in this area, and in spring it's spectacular! Teachers who want to encourage their students to protect the environment should take them – after all there's nothing like experiencing something for yourself to make you value it. We've made sure it's as accessible as possible, and hope it'll be popular with people of all ages. If you want more information, the details are all online. There's no excuse not to get out there and try it!

[pause]

tone

[The recording is repeated.]

[pause]

Question 8   *You hear a woman talking to her brother about his hair.*

[pause]

tone

Woman: It doesn't look too bad, actually.

Man: You're joking!

Woman: No way, I mean it.

Man: I think you should have taken a lot more off, especially at the front.

Woman: Well maybe you should get a hairdresser to do it instead. Though I think I did pretty well, really. Don't you think you're over-reacting a bit?

Man: I don't want all my friends to laugh at me!

Woman: They won't! Anyway, you shouldn't have it cut too often, even by me – it suits you like this. And it'll look even better in a couple of weeks.

Man: Well I suppose I should trust you ...

Woman: Of course you should! I'm your sister!

[pause]

tone

[The recording is repeated.]

[pause]

That's the end of Part One.

Now turn to Part Two.

[pause]

PART 2   *You'll hear a man called David Briggs giving a talk about his work as a volunteer on a turtle conservation programme in Western Australia. For questions 9 to 18, complete the sentences with a word or short phrase.*

You now have forty-five seconds to look at Part Two.

[pause]

tone

I want to tell you about my work as a volunteer on a turtle conservation programme this summer in Western Australia.

I'd been looking through various websites with my mother, trying, rather unsuccessfully, to find something interesting to do before I went to university when my uncle rang me and told me about this turtle tagging programme. Basically, they were asking for people to help with the actual tagging – you know, attaching electronic tags to the turtles so that scientists can collect vital data about them. So I emailed them and got all the information.

There was a choice of sites we could work at – the mainland one or the one on an island miles out into the ocean. I didn't want to be stuck right out there so my choice was easy. They wanted people who preferably had prior experience of working on conservation projects – which I hadn't – or who were keen on marine science, and that was what I was going to study at university. So that helped me get a place on the programme.

I was warned that the work would be very physical – in fact we all had to attend a medical assessment to check whether we were fit enough for the work. And there were tests to show our ability to run over longish distances – not my favourite occupation – and also whether we had the strength to lift heavy objects. Curiously, we weren't asked if we could swim, which I really thought would have been important, but I was told that most of the work took place on the beach.

The conditions offered were pretty good. Accommodation was provided and of course training, which just left me with having to pay for transport. I did think we might have to pay for food but no, all included. My mother provided me with lots of chocolate as that's one luxury she knows I can't live without. Of course, as volunteers we weren't paid for the work but that didn't really worry me.

When I got out there, I soon realised why physical fitness was important. My team had to do beach patrols at night – the female turtles come out of the ocean and on to the beach to nest then. Other volunteers worked different shifts doing other stuff in the daytime. Our patrols had to identify, tag, measure and collect data on all the turtles that were there. So you had to know what you were doing and do it fast, but what really mattered to me was to be gentle so as not to distress the turtles. Each shift lasted for about 8 hours and that might include walking up to 15 kilometres on soft sand. And on top of all that, we were operating in conditions of high humidity. I didn't enjoy the humidity but I liked the heat. The same couldn't be said for my mates on the programme, who found that hard to cope with. But we were all glad to get back to our air-conditioned huts after our shifts.

Sometimes when you were tired in the middle of a shift, it was a challenge to maintain concentration but our commitment to the project was total so our enthusiasm never seemed to flag. The scientists used the data we collected to monitor turtle behaviour, including breeding, feeding and migration patterns.

I had a good laugh with all the other volunteers when we weren't working. They were all young, but not all filling in time between school and university like me … some were unemployed. Most of them were returners, some for the sixth time. I learnt a lot about turtles and conservation issues from them. I'd consider doing it again as I thought it was a really worthwhile programme.

[pause]

Now you'll hear Part Two again.

tone

[The recording is repeated.]

[pause]

That's the end of Part Two.

Now turn to Part Three.

[pause]

PART 3   *You'll hear five short extracts in which writers give advice about writing comedy scripts for television. For questions 19 to 23, choose which piece of advice (A to H) each speaker gives. Use the letters only once. There are three extra letters which you do not need to use.*

You now have thirty seconds to look at Part Three.

[pause]

tone

Speaker 1

You have to be brutal with yourself. By that, I mean you must look carefully at what you've written and cut about half of it. Being brief and to the point is the key to writing good comedy. And listen to the rhythm of a sentence, how a joke sounds. Just removing one word, or changing its position can have a great effect. But a comedy show is more than just a series of jokes – in the best comic scenes, the humour lies in the people and how they react to their situation. So take trouble when you're creating them.

[pause]

Speaker 2

If you show viewers what they're supposed to find funny about the situation from the beginning, they have longer to enjoy it. For example, you'll get a lot of laughs if they can say straightaway, 'Oh, I see, it's a clown who doesn't like children,' or, 'Oh, I get it, it's a surgeon who can't stand the sight of blood.' And don't feel you have to explain everything in great detail – that soon gets boring. Read your script to someone with an underdeveloped sense of humour and when they start looking sleepy, you know you should cut huge chunks!

[pause]

Speaker 3

You have to be able to accept criticism. Take on board all the negative comments you get about your work and use them to improve it. I suppose it's fine if you're a brilliant writer – brilliant writers can refuse to alter their artistic vision in any way! But if, like me, you're far from being brilliant, then you need help and advice from anyone who can be bothered to give it. Not all advice is helpful, though. People often instruct young comics, 'Write about what makes you laugh,' but you won't sell many scripts if the only one to find them funny is you!

[pause]

Speaker 4

Doing any kind of writing is lonely, and comedy is no different. Finding a writing partner is great – my best days are spent sitting in a room with someone else and trying to make each other laugh. You might then have to go off and work stuff up on your own but at least you know one person has found your jokes funny! Oh, and move around a lot. It does wonders for your concentration. I've solved many problems walking to and from the fridge in search of a snack. Pausing to do a household chore, like washing up, works for other people!

[pause]

Speaker 5

The best advice I was ever given was to immerse myself in the kind of scripts that really made me laugh and to analyse how it worked. Now, I'm not telling you to copy it, but I am saying you should use it as inspiration. Then send an example of your best material to the creators of shows you admire – tell them what you admire about their work. And just keep on writing, whatever happens. At first, you might think you're mostly producing rubbish, but, gradually there will be less rubbish and more gold – so don't give up.

[pause]

Now you'll hear Part Three again.

tone

[The recording is repeated.]

[pause]

That's the end of Part Three.

Now turn to Part Four.

[pause]

PART 4   *You'll hear an interview with a woman called Maya Gardi whose daily life and business are based on waste-free principles. For questions 24 to 30, choose the best answer (A, B or C).*

You now have one minute to look at Part Four.

[pause]

tone

Interviewer: My guest this week, Maya Gardi, has recently started her own company selling environmentally-friendly products. First let me ask you, Maya, what living waste-free involves on a daily basis.

Maya: Well when I'm shopping I don't buy things in plastic packages – I take my own bags and containers and I always buy fresh local food. I compost my food rubbish and I recycle wherever I can. That kind of thing. When I started living like this, some things required a lot of adapting. My shopping habits were already pretty environmentally-friendly, although I found I had to make more of an effort to go to lots of little shops where I could choose smaller amounts more often rather than doing a single big supermarket shop every week … even though that was nice and convenient.

Interviewer: Hmm … so what made you first decide to live a completely waste-free lifestyle?

Maya: Well, I've always been quite environmentally conscious, and I think this stems from the time I read an article on the internet about all the plastic waste in our oceans. I'd pass the rubbish bins outside my block of flats and feel quite pleased that at least I wasn't throwing away as much as other people. But a few years ago, I took some stuff to my local rubbish tip to throw away … things I couldn't recycle. I was horrified at the amount of waste there. That was all it took to make me change.

Interviewer: What did your family think about your decision?

Maya: Well I live in a small flat on my own, so it wasn't as if I was imposing my lifestyle on my parents. They knew I was concerned about the environment, of course, but they still thought I was joking at first. They know how determined I am when I put my mind to something, though, and they knew that I'd be glad I'd done it.

Interviewer: So have you changed the way you prepare meals?

Maya: Well, I've never been what you'd call an expert cook, as my friends will confirm. But I'm constantly dreaming up new ways of using up bits and pieces in the fridge. I often pass on these recipes to my friends, and they're always grateful for ways to save money.

Interviewer: Does your new lifestyle make things difficult for you when you're socialising?

Maya: Yes, when I go to picnics and barbecues, for example, the plates and cutlery tend to be disposable plastic. But I have to be proactive, and not be concerned that I might come across as strange. So I would take along a proper plate, or if I couldn't do that, I'd eat from a paper napkin and then make sure it was composted rather than thrown away.

Interviewer: As you said, you've started a new business, selling environmentally-friendly products. Is it going well?

Maya: Yes, I'm selling home-made products like toothpaste and deodorant, things that are made from simple, natural ingredients. They're all sold in containers that can be recycled or returned to me. I also have an internet blog which is helping enormously with publicising my products … gives me an edge over my competitors. And I've got a few regulars I see at local events like fairs and outdoor markets. As for the future, let's see how this year goes first.

Interviewer: I hear you were also interviewed on the radio.

Maya: Yes, it was at one fair I attended. I just happened to be in the right place at the right time, when a reporter approached me. I didn't have time to get anxious! What was great was that it meant I could get my ideas across to a wider audience.

Interviewer: Thank you for your time, Maya, and best of luck for the future.

[pause]

Now you'll hear Part Four again.

tone

[The recording is repeated.]

[pause]

That's the end of Part Four.

There will now be a pause of five minutes for you to copy your answers onto the separate answer sheet. Be sure to follow the numbering of all the questions. I'll remind you when there is one minute left so that you're sure to finish in time.

[Teacher, pause the recording here for five minutes. Remind students when they have one minute left.]

That's the end of the test. Please stop now. Your supervisor will now collect all the question papers and answer sheets.

Test 3 Key

Reading and Use of English (1 hour 15 minutes)

Part 1

1 A   2 B   3 D   4 A   5 C   6 C   7 D   8 A

Part 2

9 first   10 their   11 longer   12 one   13 many
14 no/without/beyond   15 as/because/since/when   16 all

Part 3

17 discussion(s)   18 disagreement   19 length   20 existing
21 comparison   22 flight   23 impressive   24 achievement

Part 4

25 was on | his OWN
26 GAVE up (on) | reading
27 MADE it | difficult/hard for
28 did not / didn't MEAN | to leave
29 SHOULDn't / SHOULD not | have said
30 will BE two weeks | before/until/till

Part 5

31 B   32 C   33 C   34 B   35 C   36 D

Part 6

37 C   38 G   39 A   40 F   41 E   42 B

Part 7

43 B   44 D   45 A   46 D   47 A   48 C   49 C
50 A   51 C   52 A

Writing (1 hour 20 minutes)

Candidate responses are marked using the assessment scale on pages 107–108.

Listening (approximately 40 minutes)

Part 1

1 C   2 B   3 C   4 B   5 B   6 C   7 A   8 A

Part 2

9 (a) location researcher   10 (flexible) (work/working) hours / (flexibility of) (the) (work/working) hours   11 castle   12 (an) ice(-)cream / ice(-)cream(s)   13 (some) farmers   14 database   15 movie(-)map   16 leaflets   17 privacy   18 work placement (programme / program)

Part 3

19 C   20 F   21 H   22 B   23 E

Part 4

24 B   25 A   26 B   27 A   28 A   29 C   30 B

Transcript   *This is the Cambridge English: First Listening Test. Test Three.*

I'm going to give you the instructions for this test. I'll introduce each part of the test and give you time to look at the questions. At the start of each piece you will hear this sound:

tone

You'll hear each piece twice.

Remember, while you're listening, write your answers on the question paper. You'll have five minutes at the end of the test to copy your answers onto the separate answer sheet.

There will now be a pause. Please ask any questions now, because you must not speak during the test.

[pause]

Now open your question paper and look at Part One.

[pause]

PART 1   *You'll hear people talking in eight different situations. For questions 1 to 8, choose the best answer (A, B or C).*

Question 1   *You hear a young woman who is an apprentice cook talking about her apprenticeship.*

[pause]

tone

Woman: I did well at school but wasn't sure what to do next: to carry on studying, or get a job straightaway. Then I discovered the apprenticeship scheme. And now I'm in college for part of the week, studying professional cookery, and an apprentice working in local restaurants – including a four-star one – for the rest of it. The restaurant work is exhausting and, because I'm never in the same kitchen two days running, it's hard to settle into a routine. But the experience is invaluable and it's paving the way to realising my dream of opening my own restaurant. And I've learnt so many different cooking techniques from my teacher at college!

[pause]

tone

[The recording is repeated.]

[pause]

Question 2   *You hear two students talking about passing the time on bus journeys.*

[pause]

tone

Man: I seem to spend my life taking crowded buses all over town! It gets tedious and there's never a chance to sit down and do a quick bit of work.

Woman: What about music? Haven't you got any earphones?

Man: Yeah, but I suspect if I did that I'd completely lose track of time ... might miss my stop!

Woman: Oh right ... or the other thing for me is just looking out of the window at what's going on, you know, unwinding, even solving problems.

Man: I'll watch the world go by if I'm sitting in a window seat, but usually I'm jammed up against a metal pole concentrating on not losing my bag!

[pause]

tone

[The recording is repeated.]

[pause]

Question 3 *You hear a cycle coach telling his group about the ride they are going to do.*

[pause]

tone

Man: Right listen really carefully everyone. We're going to do the Moorland Hill route. Tony will lead us out of the car park. Please stay in a tight compact group with no overtaking until we get out of town and over the bridge. Then we get on to the A69 main road. We'll be turning off at the second exit, not the first … please note, because they're both signposted to Moorland Hill. I want you to try and push it up the big hill today, so save your legs and conserve some speed on the long flat stretch past Acomb village. On the return route we'll have the wind behind us, so you can get some speed up later.

[pause]

tone

[The recording is repeated.]

[pause]

Question 4 *You hear part of an interview in which a writer talks about autobiographies.*

[pause]

tone

Woman: Have you ever considered writing an autobiography?

Man: Well, certain sections of my novels are based on my experiences growing up. But, as a reader, I've found autobiographies deeply unsatisfying and have no real enthusiasm for doing one. Some consist of chapter after chapter of mind-numbing, trivial detail, or endless pages where the writer praises him or herself with little justification. Recently, in the autobiography of someone I've known personally since childhood … pure invention and no mention at all of several people who contributed significantly to his success.

[pause]

tone

[The recording is repeated.]

[pause]

Question 5   *You hear a journalist telling a colleague about her time at university.*

[pause]

tone

Man: You're a biology graduate. What prompted you to take up journalism?

Woman: You'd be amazed at how wide and varied it is and how much it overlaps with other subjects like ecology, psychology, chemistry. And you could see this from the sort of jobs biology graduates were going into – I read all this on the university website. Some were even getting into jobs like banking! As for me, I got asked to report on one of my projects for the university students' science magazine. Then that took off into a regular column, and so that sowed the seeds of a career!

[pause]

tone

[The recording is repeated.]

[pause]

Question 6   *You hear a man and a woman talking about a new clothes shop they have visited.*

[pause]

tone

Man: I went into that new clothes shop you were telling me about to have a look round.

Woman: The one in Bridge Street?

Man: Yeah, you said you really liked the way they have a member of staff just inside the door – to welcome you with a smile.

Woman: That's right. Why? Didn't you like it?

Man: Well … I can't see the point of it. And shops soon lose interest in these experiments, which tells you something about the reaction of customers. Mind you, that's a step up on what happens in some clothes shops, where you get pushy sales staff asking if you need any help the moment you get near them. That I can't stand.

[pause]

tone

[The recording is repeated.]

[pause]

Question 7   *You overhear a woman talking on the phone to a friend.*

[pause]

tone

Woman: Well, what's happening is, I'm applying for lots of full-time posts. But meanwhile I've been networking on social media with a group of recent graduates based in my town. We're planning to buy a portable climbing wall, like the things you get now in some sports centres. Then we can take it to different places where there are lots of children, like beaches, country parks, that sort of thing. Some of the guys are trained mountaineers, so the safety qualifications are already in place. And I'd be the photographer, taking action pictures of each climber to sell to the parents online. Shame it's only seasonal.

[pause]

tone

[The recording is repeated.]

[pause]

Question 8   *You hear part of a broadcast on the radio.*

[pause]

tone

Woman: A two-metre tall penguin, weighing in at 115 kilos, that's what researchers say the fossils of wing and foot bones recently unearthed in Antarctica belonged to. Such a bird would have been alive 37 million years ago. Given that the emperor penguin, the largest living species of penguin, stands 1.1 metres tall and weighs just under 50 kilos, it's no wonder that this newly discovered specimen is being called the colossus. To find out more about this extraordinary bird, including how its giant size allowed it to stay under water for up to 40 minutes to hunt for fish, tune in tonight after the weather forecast.

[pause]

tone

[The recording is repeated.]

[pause]

That's the end of Part One.

Now turn to Part Two.

[pause]

PART 2   *You'll hear a woman called Paula Kanning, who works as a film advisor in local government, talking about her work. For questions 9 to 18, complete the sentences with a word or short phrase.*

You now have forty-five seconds to look at Part Two.

[pause]

tone

Hi. I'm Paula Kanning. I work in my local council's film department. Let me explain what that is exactly. I live in a region that's featured in many films and TV programmes, and tourists are attracted there as a result. So, the local council decided to create a department with the job of promoting the region both to film-makers and to tourists who'd seen the films.

I joined the department when it was first set up. I now work as a Film Advisor, but when I started I was employed as what's called a Location Researcher. In other words, my job was to go round the region trying to identify places that'd be good for filming the outdoor sequences in films and TV programmes.

What initially attracted me to the job wasn't so much the salary, although that was OK, but the fact that it involved flexible working hours. Because I'd be travelling around the region looking for places, I could fit the work around looking after my young family.

One or two places in my region were already quite famous. For example, a big country house that once appeared in a TV drama series, and a castle that's been used in a surprising number of horror films! My job, though, was to identify less obvious places that film-makers wouldn't find without my help.

For example, I worked a lot with a company that films advertisements. They'd come to me when they wanted to film a new car zooming up a mountain road or a field of cows for a cheese advert. I didn't always find what they were looking for, but I did suggest the beach in one ice-cream advert that's been shown thousands of times in cinemas.

I spent a year in that first job – and really enjoyed it. It was fun working with the film industry, and with local people too. Locals are generally thrilled to think their village or street might feature in a film. But I remember having to spend a lot of time trying to talk farmers into allowing filming on their land.

Once I'd begun to build up a list of potential places, I decided to develop a database. This featured photos and a video clip as well as a written description of each place. I found developing all that material really rewarding and I think I did a really good job. I also made lots of useful contacts in the film industry, and films are still being made in the region as a result.

In my current job, I spend more time dealing with the tourism that films bring to the region. I get involved in the planning of projects like special weekend tours that take visitors around the places they'll recognise from films. And I'm in charge of a project called Moviemap, which is an online resource for tourists who prefer to visit the places independently.

I quite like the challenge of website design, but the tourist office also needs things to give out to tourists who aren't so keen on technology. So I also have to put together leaflets, which believe it or not is actually more complicated. I don't know why, but dealing with printers seems to involve a lot of problems.

Another thing I've been working on is a set of guidelines for tour companies which take groups of visitors to the sites – especially if it's places where people live. I think everyone understands the need to respect people's houses and land, you know, not to damage or drop litter, but people's privacy also needs to be respected.

So there's lots going on in our department – and there's only three of us working in the office. That's why we've started what's known as a work placement programme, which is aimed at young people. It involves voluntary work of course, but if we can get local teenagers in full-time education to come and work with us for a few weeks in the summer, it would help us and be great experience for them.

So before I go on to…

[pause]

Now you'll hear Part Two again.

tone

[The recording is repeated.]

[pause]

That's the end of Part Two.

Now turn to Part Three.

[pause]

PART 3   *You'll hear five short extracts in which people talk about why they didn't go to university directly after leaving school. For questions 19 to 23, choose which of the reasons (A to H) each speaker gives. Use the letters only once. There are three extra letters which you do not need to use.*

You now have thirty seconds to look at Part Three.

[pause]

tone

Speaker 1

At school, I always thought I'd wake up one day knowing exactly what I wanted to do with my life – but that never happened. I did like the idea of eventually going to university but it felt like 'same again' after 12 years of having my nose in books. When I was offered a job straight out of school, I took it without thinking. I changed jobs quite a bit before the penny finally dropped, and I realised that nursing was the career for me. I also felt that the time was right because I'd done a lot of growing up in the intervening years. So, here I am, at university at last!

[pause]

Speaker 2

Well, my wife and I got married really young – straight out of school. We just wanted to get on with being independent, I suppose, and getting on the first rung of the employment ladder was central to that. We both went out and got ourselves good positions, so financially we were secure, but after a few years, I felt I wanted to change direction in terms of my work and I realised that higher education was the only way. My wife and kids tried to persuade me to do something in computers so I could earn loads of money but I chose to do Politics instead.

[pause]

Speaker 3

When I didn't apply for a university place in my final year at school, people thought I wanted to take a year out for travelling. But I've wanted to be a vet for as long as I can remember and I especially want to treat wild animals and opportunities for studying that subject at university are few and far between. It actually took me ages to come up with one that exactly fitted the bill. Eventually, I got offered a place at a university in Europe starting next year. At least I've got time to earn a bit of money to take with me and I can hardly wait to go!

[pause]

Speaker 4

My parents dropped a bombshell when I was in my final year at school. They calmly announced that we were emigrating to Australia, where I live now! Staying behind to go to university was never an option for me cos Australia was a place I'd always fancied visiting. I think my parents just thought I'd be able to get straight into university in Australia but the system's a bit different here and it turned out I'd already missed the deadline. But I spent a great year travelling around Australia and enjoying the Australian way of life. I feel I've grown up now and become more responsible, and that I'll study harder because of my break.

[pause]

Speaker 5

I was all set to go off to university after I finished school and even had the application forms ready to fill in. Then my grandfather got taken ill and he needed help to get around. I decided to go and live with him cos my Mum was busy with a full-time job and we didn't really live nearby. So I spent six months doing that. I was completely broke but I had plenty of free time and as he lives near the sea, I even took up surfing! It was great to experience something different. He's made a full recovery now and I'm planning to go to university next year.

[pause]

Now you'll hear Part Three again.

tone

[The recording is repeated.]

[pause]

That's the end of Part Three.

Now turn to Part Four.

[pause]

PART 4   *You'll hear a radio interview with a woman called Susan Fletcher, who works on a research station in Antarctica. For questions 24 to 30, choose the best answer (A, B or C).*

You now have one minute to look at Part Four.

[pause]

tone

Interviewer: Susan Fletcher works as an environmental biologist on a research station in Antarctica. Between trips she's joined us in the studio today to talk about what it's like working in one of the remotest places on Earth.

Susan: Hi everyone!

Interviewer: First of all, you spend long periods of time in Antarctica – sometimes over a year – without coming home. How do you usually feel just before you set off?

Susan: In the days leading up to it, I feel sad of course. Everyone finds it hard to leave family behind. But I also feel grateful for having a chance to be away and I really appreciate what they mean to me. These emotions are all part of preparing, but at the same time I have to control my feelings of doubt about managing the challenges I know are coming my way.

Interviewer: You're about to leave on another trip, aren't you? Are you under a lot of pressure?

Susan: Yes, we all are. Scientists involved in polar research don't get a choice where they work, and it could be on land or at sea. To be fair we have plenty of time to get everything ready, and make sure we think of everything we'll need – both for the research and for ourselves personally. No matter how well organised a person is, though, there's always the danger of missing something that turns out to be vital, and that worry's always somewhere at the back of my mind.

Interviewer: And what are your colleagues like?

Susan: They're an amazing bunch of people, who put the interests of science and research before their own needs for months on end. Antarctica is one of the most difficult places to live on the planet, and somehow they make life there tolerable. Everyone's responsible for everyone else, and for ensuring that we achieve our objectives.

Interviewer: I suppose you have to provide your own entertainment?

Susan: Yes, indeed! Especially music evenings, or evenings when people cook food from a particular country. Although there's no shortage of enthusiasm, it has to be said that our talents lie in other fields! It's actually crucial for our wellbeing to have special events because otherwise the days just combine to become one endless day or night. In the Antarctic summer, for example, the sun rises in September, and doesn't set again until March.

Interviewer:	Is there anything you find difficult about life on a research station?
Susan:	Well it's comfortable, but it really is communal living, so you have to get used to that. We have our own bedrooms, but so much of our day is spent in other people's company, and I sometimes find that tough. By the time I get to bed at night, I'm so tired I just fall asleep immediately and sleep pretty soundly. The food's all right – you can choose what to have, and there's a reasonable variety.
Interviewer:	You obviously love your work. Can you say what it is about it that makes you want to keep on going back?
Susan:	Hmm … I mean I'm so incredibly lucky to be able to work in such an unusual environment. I walk past penguins every day, without even thinking about it. That remote and inhospitable continent miles from anywhere has come to be a second home for me, which is a real privilege.
Interviewer:	What advice would you give to students hoping to work on a research station in Antarctica in the future?
Susan:	Well there are scientists there with degrees in a wide variety of subjects from engineering to biology. And there's also a doctor, a chef, pilots, computer specialists, and people from many different walks of life. So look on the website and see what's going on. That will give you an idea of the qualifications and experience you'll need if you want to join us. You must be determined, because you'll need to become an expert in your chosen field – but if that's your dream, then go for it!
Interviewer:	Well, thanks, Susan, for telling us …

[pause]

Now you'll hear Part Four again.

tone

[The recording is repeated.]

[pause]

That's the end of Part Four.

There will now be a pause of five minutes for you to copy your answers onto the separate answer sheet. Be sure to follow the numbering of all the questions. I'll remind you when there is one minute left so that you're sure to finish in time.

[Teacher, pause the recording here for five minutes. Remind students when they have one minute left.]

That's the end of the test. Please stop now. Your supervisor will now collect all the question papers and answer sheets.

Test 4 Key

Reading and Use of English (1 hour 15 minutes)

Part 1

1 A   2 D   3 C   4 D   5 A   6 A   7 B   8 C

Part 2

9 or   10 if/should   11 What   12 its   13 as
14 Although/Though/While/Whilst   15 all   16 other

Part 3

17 employee   18 responsibility   19 division   20 significant
21 considerably   22 innovative   23 costly   24 affordable

Part 4

25 was UNABLE to land | because
26 at/on the POINT | of leaving
27 been ten years | SINCE my
28 didn't / did not say / hasn't / has not said | a WORD
29 years of AGE | may / can be / become
30 ALMOST always | on/in

Part 5

31 D   32 B   33 C   34 A   35 C   36 C

Part 6

37 E   38 C   39 G   40 B   41 D   42 F

Part 7

43 B   44 D   45 C   46 D   47 A   48 D
49 A   50 D   51 B   52 A

Writing (1 hour 20 minutes)

Candidate responses are marked using the assessment scale on pages 107–108.

Listening (approximately 40 minutes)

Part 1

1 C   2 B   3 A   4 B   5 B   6 C   7 C   8 C

Part 2

9 business (studies)   10 (natural) green(-)house   11 gallery   12 bud(s)
13 mountains   14 sandwiches   15 stream   16 winter jackets
17 nose(-)ring   18 carrots

Part 3

19 C   20 H   21 B   22 F   23 D

Part 4

24 C   25 B   26 A   27 C   28 B   29 C   30 A

Transcript   *This is the Cambridge English: First Listening Test. Test Four.*

I'm going to give you the instructions for this test. I'll introduce each part of the test and give you time to look at the questions. At the start of each piece you will hear this sound:

tone

You'll hear each piece twice.

Remember, while you're listening, write your answers on the question paper. You'll have five minutes at the end of the test to copy your answers onto the separate answer sheet.

There will now be a pause. Please ask any questions now, because you must not speak during the test.

[pause]

Now open your question paper and look at Part One.

[pause]

PART 1   *You'll hear people talking in eight different situations. For questions 1 to 8, choose the best answer (A, B or C).*

Question 1   *You hear a man talking about an ancient object he found in the ground.*

[pause]

tone

Man: It sounds silly, I know, but I'd never seen anything like that before and I just thought it was the lid of a coffee pot or something. It was disc-shaped and decorated with a snake's head on top. I was curious as I couldn't identify it, so I went along to show it to the historian in the museum in town. She looked at it and went very quiet. It was at that point I realised that I'd found something really special. She entered it into a register of local historical finds and then sent it off to the National Museum and it's still there now in an exhibition!

[pause]

tone

[The recording is repeated.]

[pause]

Question 2   *You hear two friends talking about advertising.*

[pause]

tone

Man: Have you seen that new mobile phone ad?

Woman: Oh yeah, it's everywhere. It's quite fun, though I can't say I feel that way about most advertisements.

Man: Some of them are very clever, though, aren't they?

Woman: Yes, when it comes to persuading people they can't live without stuff that's actually completely useless! Or at least they usually already have something just as good, so why replace it?

Man: But it's interesting to know what's out there, isn't it?

Woman: Well I'd say there are better ways of finding out about whether new products are any good than believing an ad that's cost millions to make!

Man: Yeah, maybe, but they don't do any harm, really.

[pause]

tone

[The recording is repeated.]

[pause]

Question 3   *You hear an actor talking about her career.*

[pause]

tone

Woman: I went for an audition to get into drama school cos I'd always wanted to be an actor. Anyway, they turned me down, which was a major obstacle. While I was trying to decide what to do next with my life, I went out for a meal with an old friend of mine who's a successful actor, to ask her for some advice. So we were sitting in this restaurant chatting away when a film director came up to say hello. My friend'd worked with him on a film and introduced me. A few days later, the director just phoned up and offered me a role in his next film!

[pause]

tone

[The recording is repeated.]

[pause]

Question 4   *You hear a tour guide telling a group of tourists about a view.*

[pause]

tone

Woman: Let me just stop here to enable you to savour the spectacular view. So over to your left, if you look down you can see a little circular wood. Well that's quite a famous landmark locally because the poet Francis Alder actually used to have a cabin in that wood. Now down in the valley below there you can make out the River Thorn at its widest point, which Alder actually wrote about in many of his poems we all read when we were at school. Then if you look to halfway up the hill I'm sure you can see a large green area known as Callaway Park that's popular with young families.

[pause]

tone

[The recording is repeated.]

[pause]

Question 5	*You hear a man talking to a friend about a presentation he has just given.*

[pause]

tone

Woman: So, how did your presentation go?

Man: Pretty well, I think ... and judging by the number of people there, I'd picked the right topic. It's an area of law that's very relevant at the moment, and that was reflected in the size of the audience. So I needn't have worried on that score. All that practising in front of the mirror paid off, as did all that work I did recording myself and making sure I could easily be heard at the back of the room. I was quite well prepared for the questions, though of course there were a couple I hadn't expected – there always are.

[pause]

tone

[The recording is repeated.]

[pause]

Question 6	*You hear two students talking about a careers talk they have just heard at college.*

[pause]

tone

Woman: That was a good careers talk, wasn't it?

Man: Well, yes and no. I mean, the speaker knew his stuff, but not much of it was new – we've already had two careers talks this year, covering most of the same topics.

Woman: Hmm ... you have a point there, but he made some great jokes, and held everyone's attention. There was no chatting in the back row, or people checking their phones every five minutes.

Man: Actually, there was quite a lot of that – I think you just didn't notice. I did think he was funny, though.

[pause]

tone

[The recording is repeated.]

[pause]

Question 7   *You hear an author of children's books talking about her work.*

[pause]

tone

Woman: When I start writing a novel for children, my main aim is not to write a successful book – I write about things that I used to love reading about when I was their age. I've been writing novels for children for some years now and I've come to realise that mystery is important, but, what the children really want to read about is the young characters in the book. By solving a mystery, the characters have to build their relationships and solve problems together. So many writers try to teach children things too directly, but doing that just turns children off.

[pause]

tone

[The recording is repeated.]

[pause]

Question 8   *You hear a man and a woman talking about older people learning languages.*

[pause]

tone

Man: How are your mum's Spanish classes going?

Woman: Oh, I'm not sure. She thinks she's too old to be doing them. The younger students learn so much quicker than her.

Man: Younger students do pick things up more quickly in terms of accent and so on. But I think older people have an advantage. They've learnt to be efficient in how they spend their time and they've also learnt how to study. I bet your mum's grammar and vocabulary are better than the younger students'. Anyway, there are so many apps and programmes out there for learning languages so people of any age can practise their skills whenever they want – even on the way to work!

[pause]

tone

[The recording is repeated.]

[pause]

That's the end of Part One.

Now turn to Part Two.

[pause]

PART 2 | *You'll hear a student called Andy Richards talking about his recent trip to the tea growing region of Assam in Northern India. For questions 9 to 18, complete the sentences with a word or short phrase.*

You now have forty-five seconds to look at Part Two.

[pause]

tone

Hello. I'm Andy Richards and I'm here to talk about my recent trip to a tea plantation in the north-east of India, where Assam tea is grown.

My trip to the tea plantation was for my first year university project. If you're not a business studies student, you might wonder why I chose that destination – after all, you'd think it would better suit natural sciences or geography students – but luckily I found lots that related to my course and my project.

On the first morning of the visit, we were given a talk by the plantation manager about how the tea's grown. I discovered that the region where it's grown is really hot and experiences high rainfall. The humidity traps the heat in and provides perfect growing conditions – a kind of natural greenhouse if you like. It certainly felt like one anyway!

After the talk, we were invited to a tea tasting session. We went along the veranda of the plantation house and into the dining room. On the other side was a separate room called the gallery and this was where the tea tasting took place. Awaiting us was a range of fifty-seven different types of tea blends from around the world.

Then, we went on a tour of the plantation and saw the tea pickers who were mainly women. They were amazingly fast and skilful. They used their thumbs and forefingers to pick the buds and leaves from the stem of the tea plant. I was surprised because I thought only the leaves would get picked. I got to ask a lot of questions about the commercial aspects of the plantation for my project.

To finish off a fantastic first day, a special afternoon tea complete with elephant ride had been organised. I had a fantastic view from the elephant's back and I was amazed that I was able to catch a glimpse of the mountains on the horizon. We wandered along the roads and through the local villages, watching the local people going about their daily lives.

Eventually, we arrived at a neighbouring tea garden where refreshments were waiting for us. We had sandwiches that literally melted in your mouth – why don't they taste like that at home? We also tried some curry puffs and some cream cakes … a speciality of the area apparently. And there was tea too obviously!

After a while, the sun began to go down and we could choose how to get back to the plantation. Some chose to walk or go by elephant. I decided to ride a vintage motorbike back, which meant driving through the villages on a muddy track. I was OK until I tried to cross a stream. The tyres slipped on the stones, but luckily I only got my feet wet!

We were lucky that our two-day visit coincided with the Saturday market in the nearest village. I was surprised at how big it was and I spent several hours wandering down the narrow aisles between the stalls looking at the jewellery, the colourful saris and believe it or not – the winter jackets! That was rather puzzling considering the weather!

I had a go at bargaining for the best price for some presents. I was a bit embarrassed to begin with. I started off buying a bag for my older sister. I probably paid too much to be honest but later I bought a nose ring for my other sister – and by then I'd really got into it! I think I got a real bargain there!

Everything was larger than life in that market – especially the food … nothing like shopping in a supermarket back home. The red peppers looked as if they'd been polished, the colourful spices were overflowing out of large sacks and the carrots were bright red too, twice the size I'm used to, so I actually bought some of those – tasted amazing.

Now let me move on to the lavish dinner they prepared.

[pause]

Now you'll hear Part Two again.

tone

[The recording is repeated.]

[pause]

That's the end of Part Two.

Now turn to Part Three.

[pause]

PART 3

You'll hear five short extracts in which people are talking about work they did in shops. For questions 19 to 23, choose from the options (A to H) what each person says about their experience. Use the letters only once. There are three extra letters which you do not need to use.

You now have thirty seconds to look at Part Three.

[pause]

tone

Speaker 1

I spent six months as a sales assistant in a toy shop. Until you've actually done it, you don't realise how hard it is, working in a shop. They say the customers are always right but let me tell you, they're not! Sometimes they're simply rude. When I'd had a particularly tough day for one reason or another, my fellow workers were always sympathetic, for which I was very grateful. But I was glad it was only a temporary job, even though I was quite good at it. One thing came as a result of that … I'm always nice to shop assistants now!

[pause]

Speaker 2

The shop where I worked sold mobile phones. There were six of us working there and there was never a moment when we weren't rushing about. It's draining being on your feet all day. Some of our customers hadn't a clue what they wanted and others seemed to have a lot more knowledge than me. You had to be ready for a huge variety of questions. At the end of my shift, my brain couldn't cope with any more! In the evenings I just sat at home watching rubbish on the TV. I work in a flower shop now – much more my thing!

[pause]

Speaker 3

I sold jeans in a really fashionable shop. We worked on commission, which made selling quite competitive, so the more I sold the bigger my take-home pay was. Even knowing that, I couldn't make myself push a pair of jeans on a customer if I thought they looked awful on her. And I think the customers recognised my honesty because I had a lot coming back who chose to be served by me. It was quite satisfying knowing that my approach seemed to work. In the end, I probably sold just as many as my colleagues, if not more.

[pause]

Speaker 4

My colleagues were great and I really enjoyed some aspects of selling. I mean, I knew I was a good sales assistant, even with difficult customers. I was working in a furniture shop selling top-of-the-range sofas and chairs. In fact, we were also having to sell some stuff that wasn't top of the range, and that wasn't reflected in the price. I tried to put people off buying these lower quality pieces as I didn't think they were worth the money. In the end, I left because of this and I've moved out of selling. I miss it sometimes.

[pause]

Speaker 5

The dress shop I worked in always seemed to be having a sale where loads of things were marked down by as much as 50%. It attracted customers into the shop but not much of the discounted stuff was sold. Customers preferred our latest models, which were full price. But I wasn't very good with customers. I'd had a couple of days before I started with the manager who went through the stock with me and the mysteries of the credit card machine but nothing on actually dealing with customers. So I left after a couple of months and tried something else instead.

[pause]

Now you'll hear Part Three again.

tone

[The recording is repeated.]

[pause]

That's the end of Part Three.

Now turn to Part Four.

[pause]

PART 4   *You'll hear an interview with Marvin Benby, a beekeeper who keeps his bees in hives on a city rooftop. For questions 24 to 30, choose the best answer (A, B or C).*

You now have one minute to look at Part Four.

[pause]

tone

Interviewer:	I'm talking to Marvin Benby, a city beekeeper. Marvin, how did you get into this?
Marvin:	I'd always been interested in insects, and a friend in the countryside was always telling me how enjoyable he found beekeeping. He's got his own hives, you know, beehives, which bees are kept in, and produces beautiful honey, but living in a city, doing it myself hadn't occurred to me – where would I keep them? I knew so little about it. Then I saw a newspaper ad for a beekeeping workshop, and told my friend ... but he just raised his eyebrows. That was it – I thought 'you don't believe I can do it', and signed up for the course.
Interviewer:	Is keeping bees fun?
Marvin:	Well, I've become somewhat obsessed with bees. As you probably know, they're essential for keeping plants growing. They help spread their seeds. You're doing a favour to society by keeping up bee numbers, providing homes for them. Of course, my friends love me because I'm always giving them pots of honey. You only open the hive for a good reason, as it's an intrusion breaking the seal on the hive. It's the highlight for me and I can hardly sleep the night before – looking forward to seeing how they're doing.
Interviewer:	Is it difficult keeping bees in a city?
Marvin:	Wherever you do it you'll have to invest in things – a honey extractor, a bee smoker, special gear to protect yourself – the stuff's as easy to get in urban as in rural areas. It's devastating if a disease strikes the hive – you can't help but feel responsible, even if it's just nature taking its course. Actually bees in rural areas suffer worse – many say it's due to pesticides used on farm crops. In fact city bees are fortunate enough to be exposed to a tremendous diversity of plants. There are things growing everywhere.
Interviewer:	Do your neighbours mind you keeping bees?
Marvin:	I'm lucky to have some roof space where my beehives sit – my neighbours don't seem to mind. I wondered if there'd be complaints as some people worry about the fact bees can sting. But they only sting if they feel threatened. I originally kept the hives at street level, but then offered to move them up to the roof when I discovered the guy who lives on the ground floor's allergic to them. He mentioned the risks and it seemed wiser to relocate to the top of the building.
Interviewer:	This is your fifth year of beekeeping ...

Marvin: Yes ... I'll never forget setting up my first hive. It involved moving my bees from a box into a new wooden hive. It's important they don't have any confusion about where the entrance to the new hive is – it must be in a familiar position or they get lost if they fly outside. I had to feed the bees sugar syrup, so they'd be full and sleepy, and wouldn't react badly. I'd forgotten to bring gloves, and as I poured in the sugar syrup, to make matters worse, I spilt some on my unprotected hands, so they were sticky, and bees started settling on them. I was terrified they'd turn agitated and aggressive, but it went smoothly.

Interviewer: You now sell honey and candles made from beeswax ...

Marvin: ... and other products. I had to put quite a bit of cash down for stuff I needed, but I'm determined to turn it into a profitable business, and I've recruited some volunteers to help me sell things. I'm keen to involve the local community as much as possible ... hopefully more people will consider taking up beekeeping – everyone loves honey after all!

Interviewer: So, what's next ...?

Marvin: My knowledge has reached a point where ideally I'd say I'm confident enough to sit back a bit more in the coming months, which is what an experienced beekeeper hopes to do when things are going well. There's little certainty though ... the next season brings fear as well as hope and joy ... if you lose bees, there's guilt, did you do something wrong? The weather's definitely key too – how the bees manage it affects everything.

[pause]

Now you'll hear Part Four again.

tone

[The recording is repeated.]

[pause]

That's the end of Part Four.

There will now be a pause of five minutes for you to copy your answers onto the separate answer sheet. Be sure to follow the numbering of all the questions. I'll remind you when there is one minute left so that you're sure to finish in time.

[Teacher, pause the recording here for five minutes. Remind students when they have one minute left.]

That's the end of the test. Please stop now. Your supervisor will now collect all the question papers and answer sheets.

CAMBRIDGE ENGLISH
Language Assessment
Part of the University of Cambridge

Do not write in this box

SAMPLE

Candidate Name
If not already printed, write name in CAPITALS and complete the Candidate No. grid (in pencil).

Candidate Signature ....

Examination Title

Centre

Supervisor:
If the candidate is ABSENT or has WITHDRAWN shade here ⊏⊐

Centre No.

Candidate No.

Examination Details

0 0 0 0
1 1 1 1
2 2 2 2
3 3 3 3
4 4 4 4
5 5 5 5
6 6 6 6
7 7 7 7
8 8 8 8
9 9 9 9

Candidate Answer Sheet

Instructions

Use a PENCIL (B or HB).

Rub out any answer you wish to change using an eraser.

Parts 1, 5, 6 and **7:**
Mark ONE letter for each question.

For example, if you think **B** is the right answer to the question, mark your answer sheet like this:

0 | A | B̸ | C | D

Parts 2, 3 and **4:**
Write your answer clearly in CAPITAL LETTERS.

For Parts 2 and 3 write one letter in each box. For example:

0 | E X A M P L E

Part 1

1	A	B	C	D
2	A	B	C	D
3	A	B	C	D
4	A	B	C	D
5	A	B	C	D
6	A	B	C	D
7	A	B	C	D
8	A	B	C	D

Part 2

Do not write below here

9		9 1 0 u
10		10 1 0 u
11		11 1 0 u
12		12 1 0 u
13		13 1 0 u
14		14 1 0 u
15		15 1 0 u
16		16 1 0 u

Continues over ➡

FCE R

DP802

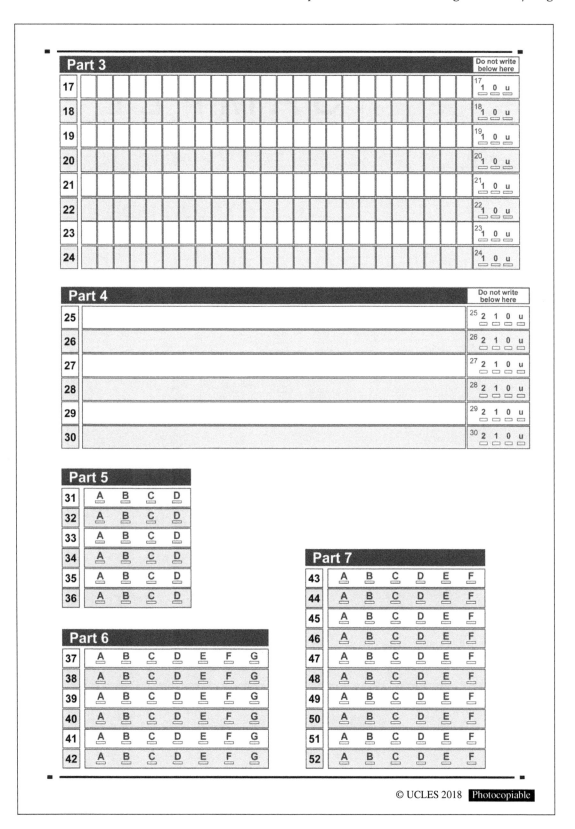

Sample answer sheet: Listening

CAMBRIDGE ENGLISH
Language Assessment
Part of the University of Cambridge

Do not write in this box

SAMPLE

Candidate Name
If not already printed, write name
in CAPITALS and complete the
Candidate No. grid (in pencil).

Candidate Signature

Examination Title

Centre

Supervisor:
If the candidate is ABSENT or has WITHDRAWN shade here ⊂⊐

Centre No.

Candidate No.

**Examination
Details**

Candidate Answer Sheet

Instructions

Use a PENCIL (B or HB).
Rub out any answer you wish to change using an eraser.

Parts 1, 3 and **4**:
Mark ONE letter for each question.

For example, if you think **B** is the
right answer to the question, mark
your answer sheet like this:

Part 2:
Write your answer clearly in CAPITAL LETTERS.

Write one letter or number in each box.
If the answer has more than one word, leave one
box empty between words.

For example:

Turn this sheet over to start.

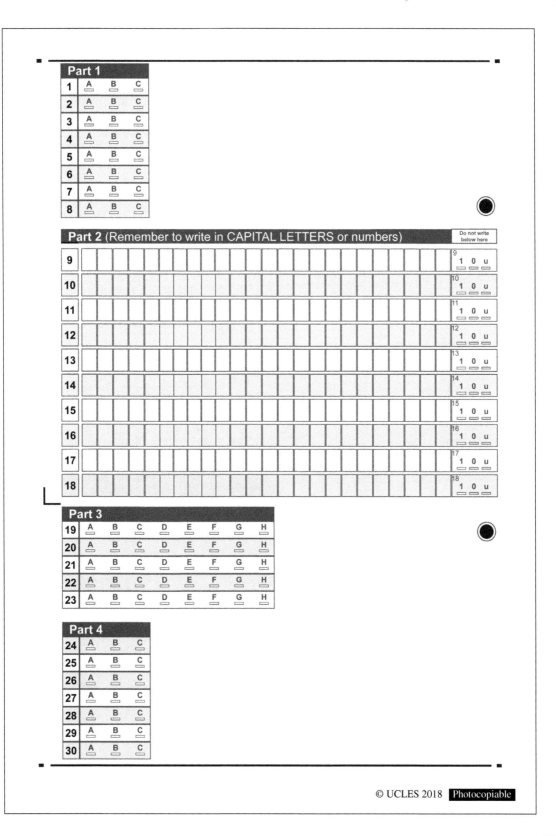

Acknowledgements

The authors and publishers acknowledge the following sources of copyright material and are grateful for the permissions granted. While every effort has been made, it has not always been possible to identify the sources of all the material used, or to trace all copyright holders. If any omissions are brought to our notice, we will be happy to include the appropriate acknowledgements on reprinting and in the next update to the digital edition, as applicable.

Key: T = Top; B = Below.

Text

Heston Blumenthal for the text on p. 14 adapted from In Search of Total Perfection by Heston Blumenthal. Published by Bloomsbury. Copyright © 2009 Henston Blumenthal. Reproduced by permission of the author c/o Rogers, Colerdige & White Ltd. 20 Powis Mews, London W11 1JN; Travel Mamas for the text on p. 16 adapted from 'Swimming with Manatees, Florida's Gentle Giants' by Bel Kembach, 25.04.2017. Copyright © 2017 Travel Mamas. Reproduced with kind permission; Guardian News & Media Limited for the text on p. 19 adapted from 'Madagascar's fishing villagers learn to survive by managing their stocks' by Kit Buchan, The Guardian, 05.05.2015. Copyright © Guardian News and Media Limited 2015. Reproduced with permission; Guardian News & Media Limited for the text on p. 19 adapted from 'Cheap solar lamps help villagers keep their health, and cut emissions' by Katie Forster, The Guardian, 05.05.2015. Copyright © Guardian News and Media Limited 2015. Reproduced with permission; Guardian News & Media Limited for the text on p. 19 adapted from 'Vietnam cities told that driving down pollution is a matter of ride-sharing' by Kit Buchan, The Guardian, 05.05.2015. Copyright © Guardian News and Media Limited 2015. Reproduced with permission; Guardian News & Media Limited for the text on p. 19 adapted from 'Ghanas's bicycle which is creating jobs while it saves the soil' by Corinne Jones, The Guardian, 05.05.2015. Copyright © Guardian News and Media Limited 2015. Reproduced with permission; Guardian News & Media Limited for the text on p. 36 adapted from 'How do I become…a guitar maker?' by Sandra Haurant, The Guardian, 18.11.2015. Copyright © Guardian News and Media Limited 2015. Reproduced with permission; Guardian News & Media Limited for the text on p. 38 adapted from 'The BBC's Operation Iceberg captures a brief moment frozen in time' by Helen Czerski, The Guardian, 29.10.2012. Copyright © Guardian News and Media Limited 2012. Reproduced with permission; Telegraph Media Group Limited for the text on p. 41 adapted from 'Follow your animal instincts to keep fit' by Annabel Vennin, The Telegraph, 29.11.2014. Copyright © 2014 Telegraph Media Group Limited. Reproduced with permission; Telegraph Media Group Limited for the text on p. 58 adapted from 'Brother of all challenges for Alistair Brownlee' by Dominic Utton, The Telegraph, 13.02.2015. Copyright © 2015 Telegraph Media Group Limited. Reproduced with permission; Macmillan Publishers Limited for the text on p. 60 adapted from 'Dam removals: Rivers on the run' by Richard A. Lovett, Nature Vol. 511 Issue 7511, 30.07.2014. Copyright © 2014 Macmillan Publishers Limited. Reproduced with permission via the Copyright Clearance Center; Guardian News & Media Limited for the text on p. 63 adapted from 'What is it like to quit your life and start again?' by Becky Barnicoat and Chris Broughton, The Guardian, 12.06.2015. Copyright © Guardian News and Media Limited 2015. Reproduced with permission; Kalmbach Publishing Co. for the text on p. 74 from 'Archaeologists Find Earliest Evidence of Humans Cooking With Fire' by Kenneth Miller, 17.12.2013. Copyright © 2013 Kalmbach Publishing Co. Reproduced with kind permission; Telegraph Media Group Limited for the text on p. 80 adapted from 'My winter on a husky farm in the Arctic Circle' by Cal Flyn, The Telegraph, 20.12.2013. Copyright © Telegraph Media Group Limited. Reproduced with permission; Guardian News & Media Limited for the text on p. 82 from 'The man who feeds the developing world's children from a garden shed' by Joanna Moorhead, 17.05.2015. Copyright © Guardian News & Media Limited 2015. Reproduced with permission; Susannah Butter for the text on p. 85 from 'A day in the life of … An Evening Standard journalist' by Susannah Butter, The Reading Agency website. Copyright © 2013 Susannah Butter. Reproduced with kind permission.

Photos

All the photographs are sourced from Getty Images.

p. C1 (T): Witold Skrypczak/Witold Skrypczak; p. C1 (B): Daniel Allan/Daniel Allan; p. C2 (T): FRED TANNEAU/AFP; p. C2 (B): Ascent/PKS Media Inc./The Image Bank; p. C4 (T): Richard Baker/In Pictures; p. C4 (B): Maskot; p. C5 (T): Katrina Wittkamp/DigitalVision; p. C5 (B), p. C8 (B): Hero Images; p. C7 (T): Monty Rakusen/Cultura; p. C7 (B): PeopleImages/DigitalVision; p. C8 (T): Chris Cross/Caiaimage; p. C10 (T): Jordan Siemens/DigitalVision; p. C10 (B): Image Source; p. C11 (T): franckreporter/E+; p. C11 (B): Glowimages.

Visual materials for the Speaking test

Why are the people getting information about these things?

1A

1B

Why are the people walking in these places?

1C

1D

1E

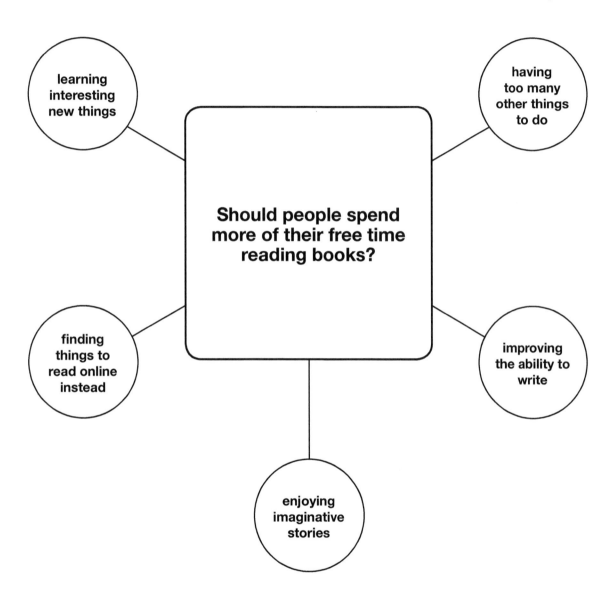

learning interesting new things

having too many other things to do

Should people spend more of their free time reading books?

finding things to read online instead

improving the ability to write

enjoying imaginative stories

What are the people enjoying about spending their holidays in these ways?

2A

2B

What might the people find difficult about choosing things in these situations?

2C

2D

2E

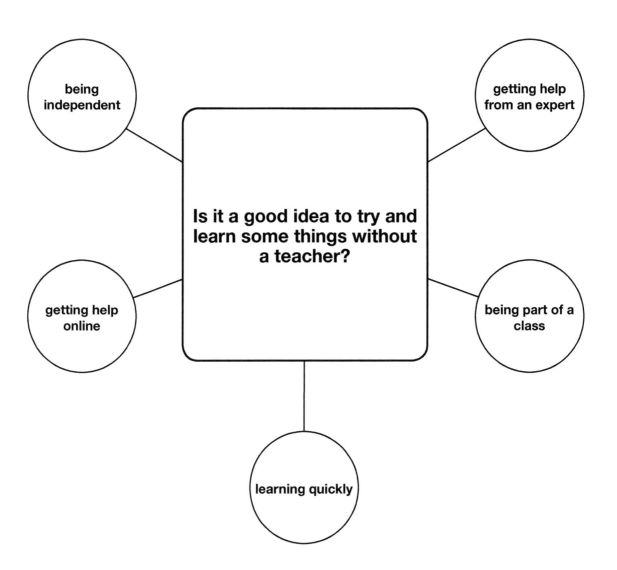

being independent

getting help from an expert

Is it a good idea to try and learn some things without a teacher?

getting help online

being part of a class

learning quickly

Why have the people decided to use their phones in these situations?

3A

3B

What are the people enjoying about doing these winter activities?

3C

3D

3E

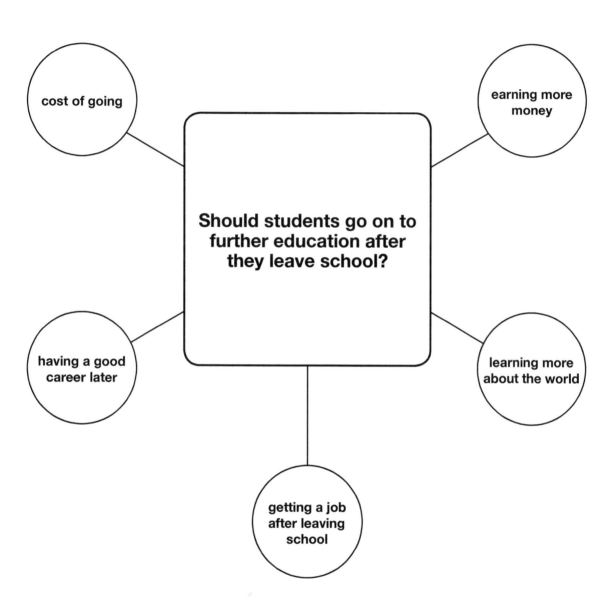

What are the people enjoying about spending time in these beautiful places?

4A

4B

Why are the people listening to music in these situations?

4C

4D

4E

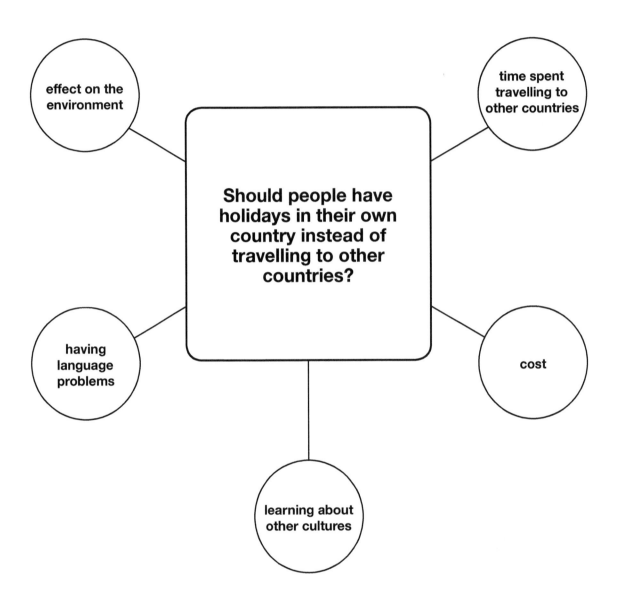

effect on the environment

time spent travelling to other countries

Should people have holidays in their own country instead of travelling to other countries?

having language problems

cost

learning about other cultures

Cambridge English

OFFICIAL EXAM PREPARATION MATERIALS

CAMBRIDGE.ORG/EXAMS

What do we do?

Together, Cambridge University Press and Cambridge English Language Assessment bring you official preparation materials for Cambridge English exams and IELTS.

What does *official* mean?

Our authors are experts in the exams they write for. In addition, all of our exam preparation is officially validated by the teams who produce the real exams.

Why else are our materials special?

Vocabulary is always 'on-level' as defined by the English Profile resource. Our materials are based on research from the Cambridge Learner Corpus to help students avoid common mistakes that exam candidates make.

Authentic examination papers: what do we mean?

PRETESTING

INVOLVING
WRITING TEAMS
AROUND THE WORLD

VALIDATION

PRACTICE
PAPERS

◀ — SELECTION — ▶

LIVE
EXAMS

Testbank

NOW ALSO AVAILABLE
ONLINE IN Testbank

Practice makes perfect!